Talking Your Way to Success—
the Story of
the Dale Carnegie Course

Talking Your Way to Success—
the Story of
The Dale Carnegie Course

TALKING
your way to
SUCCESS –

Association Press
New York

the
story
of
the
DALE
CARNEGIE
COURSE

WILLIAM LONGGOOD

TALKING YOUR WAY TO SUCCESS—
THE STORY OF THE DALE CARNEGIE COURSE

Copyright © 1962 by
National Board of Young Men's Christian Associations

Association Press, 291 Broadway, New York 7, N.Y.

First Printing 1962
Second Printing 1969
Third Printing 1973

Library of Congress catalog card number: 62–9393

Publisher's title stock number: 1475

Printed in the United States of America

Foreword

The happiest and most satisfying period of my adult life dates from the time of my association with Dale Carnegie and the Dale Carnegie Course. That involvement began as a job, progressed to marriage, and ended with total commitment both to the man and the movement. Since the death of my husband in 1955, it has been my task to continue his work and expand its influence. This responsibility has not replaced my sense of personal loss but it has channeled it into dedicated activity and given direction to what is left of my life.

My feeling, then, about this book is necessarily intense and biased—I am too close to its subject to appraise it objectively. I do know, however, that Mr. William Longgood, the author, has made a tremendous effort to study, research, and analyze the Dale Carnegie Course from the standpoint of an unprejudiced observer. My organization, Dale Carnegie & Associates, Inc., has aided him by opening our classrooms and our files and by leaving him free to pursue his investigations in his own way and to draw his own conclusions and interpretations.

Mr. Longgood, in my opinion, has succeeded brilliantly in assessing the underlying psychological principles which are at work in the Dale Carnegie Course. His perception and understanding of these forces are keen and shrewdly observed.

I wish he had known Dale Carnegie personally, in order to convey something of the warmth, charm, and humor of his lively, sparkling self. The mere facts of Dale's life and work can never explain or recreate that electric, radiant personality who loved life, people, and his chosen work.

I am deeply grateful to Mr. Longgood and to Association Press for recognizing Dale Carnegie's lifework as a significant contribution to the world we live in. The best memorial to his success, as the title of this book indicates, is seen in the lives of his many students over the world who have, through him, learned to live with more courage, confidence, and fulfillment and to develop a deeper awareness of the possibilities in themselves and others. As long as we keep these goals uppermost in continuing his work, the Dale Carnegie Course will still retain its unique position in our society as a force for good.

Dorothy Carnegie

Contents

x

I.
THE FACES

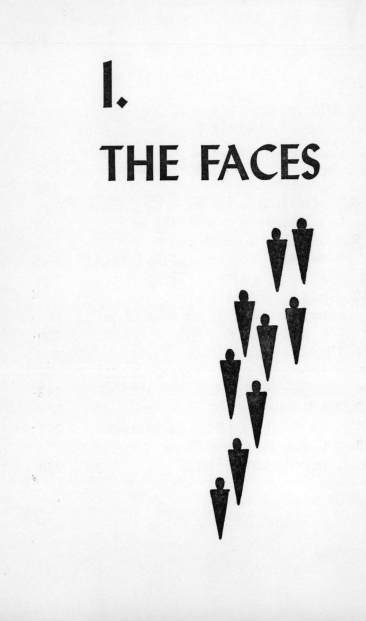

OF SUCCESS

Reflecting in a Man
and a Movement

SHORTLY AFTER Dale Carnegie's famous book, *How to Win Friends and Influence People*, appeared in 1936, a magazine published a cartoon showing a group of people on a railroad bar car with their arms thrown around one another, laughing hilariously and slapping each other on the back in an outrageous display of conviviality. The caption explained, "Dale Carnegie just got off at Albuquerque."

13

In the wake of that celebrated cartoon and others playing on the same theme, *How to Win Friends and Influence People* went on to become high on the list of the top ten best sellers of all time, having sold over six million copies to date.

The cartoon cited above, a favorite of Carnegie's, was part of what is probably the greatest barrage of satire, mockery, ridicule, sharp-shooting, savage thrusts, and good-natured jibes ever leveled at a publication. It even triggered a book-length burlesque with the apposite title, *How to Lose Friends and Alienate People*, with a mocking picture of its author, Irving Tressler, on the dust jacket, complete with handle-bar mustache. The Tressler book was a prized exhibit in Carnegie's collection of humor at his expense.

An invidious moral could be drawn from the fate of the two authors: Carnegie, after a rich life and a successful career, died at his home in Forest Hills, Long Island, in 1955 of natural causes at age 67, optimistic, happy, and vibrant almost to the end. Tressler, when only 35, committed suicide in 1944; his obituary noted ironically that he was best known for his take-off on *How to Win Friends and Influence People*.

Typical of the Tressler book, dedicated "to the man who doesn't need to read it—Adolph Hitler," was this burlesque of the Carnegie offering:

If you wish to get the most out of this book there is one major requirement, in addition to being able to read and understand words of more than four letters. What is this magic requirement? Just this: a deep, driving desire to want to make others dislike you, just as much as you dislike them, a vigorous determination to recognize the fact that most people are about as interesting as a semi-annual report of the U.S. Gypsum Co.

"He who is rich in friends is poor in privacy."

While the Tressler book, and most of the other rollicking thrusts at Carnegie made delightful reading, they had an unfortunate result: Dale Carnegie and his methods became completely distorted in the public mind. His name was often used synonymously with insincerity, and his methods were equated with manipulating people by sinister psychological means for selfish ends.

This image, as it is referred to in Madison Avenue advertising circles, has persisted, but in recent years has begun to soften and give way to a truer picture of Carnegie's aims and ideals under the impact of an enormous advertising and promotional campaign, and an ever-swelling army of graduates of the Dale Carnegie Course in Effective Speaking and Human Relations, who march forth with about the same zeal as missionaries setting out to bring light to the heathen.

This may sound like a curious or farfetched analogy unless one understands the powerful impact the Carnegie course has had on many lives. The course involves much more than merely mastering the simple skill of giving a talk before a group of people without fainting, suffering an attack of gastronomical butterflies, or having the knees pound together like castanets; it involves more than just memorizing a few ground rules designed to promote better relations with other people. The basic principle is founded on the life experiences each class member has had, reaching deep into the mind, heart, and wellspring of human experience.

On a typical evening in a Dale Carnegie class, one student told how he struck his wife while teaching her to drive a car and how it affected their marriage; another recalled the happy memory of a family outing in childhood; a third talked about the frustrations of a marriage-minded single girl in a big city.

A dentist told how lack of self-confidence prevented him from breaking up an unsatisfactory partnership with another dentist, and how he would lie on his bed worrying for hours about how he would send his children through college twenty years hence. A clerk told about his problems with an unsympathetic boss. A young woman recalled how she grieved over the loss of her mother. In more extraordinary circumstances, a bachelor related the torment he suffered after getting a girl pregnant.

A New York advertising account executive, a man in his mid-forties, told how he almost took his own life. He said that for six months prior to enrolling in the course he felt depressed and couldn't rise from his black mood. Everything went wrong for him; he lost a valuable account, his wife was considering divorce, his children no longer were close to him. The classroom was taut as he told his story:

" 'Why go on?' I asked myself. 'I have no real home life. No one loves me or cares what happens to me.'

"I bought a gun, determined to shoot myself. But I was determined not to frighten my children any more than necessary and not to let it be messy. I wanted to go out in dignity. So I dressed myself in clean linen, clean shirt, a freshly pressed suit. Then I took my revolver and went to the bathroom.

"I decided the easiest thing to do was to sit in the bathtub to perform the last act of my life. I climbed slowly into the tub, adjusted my clothes, took out the gun and debated how to proceed. If I shot myself through the head, blood would splatter the walls. So I decided to shoot myself in the chest.

"As I made my decision, there was a sharp rap on

the door and a shrill cry from my younger son: 'Daddy, I've got to go to the bathroom.'

"I didn't answer. My son pounded harder on the door. My wife shouted, 'Harold, you get out of there and let him in.'

"It was disconcerting: the most dramatic moment of my life and people were talking about using the bathroom. But I was determined to go through with it. I told myself I was going to count to three and pull the trigger.

"One . . .

"Two . . .

"I closed my eyes, my finger tightened slowly on the trigger—when suddenly my older boy began hammering on the bathroom door with both fists, shouting that he had to get in right away. As the two boys stood outside pounding on the door and shouting, and my wife hollering at me to get out, I said the hell with it, put the gun away, and let the kids in.

"I'm practically a teetotaler, but I was shaking so that I went downstairs and poured myself a triple shot. I sat down and thought about what I'd almost done, about my problems. My trouble was that I had no formula to help me handle my difficulties. . . ."

The ad man said that in the next few weeks there was an upturn in his fortunes, and on the advice of a friend he enrolled in the Dale Carnegie Course. He concluded on a high note, pointing out that through the training he had gained a new perspective toward life and himself and was able to cope with his problems.

This type of melodrama is not the usual fare served up by the speakers, but students often tell intimate facts about themselves that one would not expect to hear in a public gathering. More remarkable, in the context of the course they usually do not seem extraordinary.

Most incidents that unfold are ordinary events in the lives of ordinary people, but frequently there is a leavening of humor.

The nature of the course itself is responsible for such intimate revelations. In the Dale Carnegie method, effective speaking is merely a vehicle which enables people to see themselves and the world in a new perspective. The defunct *Collier's* magazine (January 15, 1949) stated:

As practiced in a Carnegie class, where every student must take his turn on the rostrum, public speaking is group therapy not unlike that practiced by Alcoholics Anonymous. By teaching his students to speak easily before a group, Carnegie has saved as many people from their own dread uncertainties as Alcoholics Anonymous has saved from the whiskey barrel.

The Carnegie people do not claim that the course is

anything more than an effective speaking and human relations workshop, but it is undeniable that strong psychological forces are at work. The basic idea behind the course is that people's attitudes can be changed, and if they are guided and directed intelligently the inevitable result will be beneficial. The change in attitude is brought about in such subtle ways that often it isn't as apparent to the person directly affected as to those he lives and works with.

Most talks—they are never called speeches—must be based on something the speaker has "earned the right" to talk about—an experience he has lived through. When a person starts probing within himself, examining his attitudes and feelings, he often comes up with some startling discoveries about himself; for most students the course is an adventure in self-discovery.

A New York boy, a teen-ager, disclosed that he had lived in anguish, hating his father and mother. He explained that he couldn't talk to them, although he lived at home with both parents, because many years earlier he and a companion had gone to his attic and gotten into a candy box containing family souvenirs. Along with his father's old war medals were a Catholic marriage certificate and the boy's birth certificate.

His friend pointed out a discrepancy in the dates of the two documents and taunted him about being a bastard.

"I couldn't speak to my parents about this," the youth said, "but I hated them for it." While attending the course he discovered that his attitude had been wrong and that he had within himself the courage to talk to his mother. She explained that she and the boy's father had been married during World War II in a civil ceremony, and after the war they had the belated Catholic wedding.

As classes progress, the student gradually breaks down his fear of speaking and gains self-confidence. This often leads to remarkable results in releasing the total personality, especially when the human relations principles are applied; for many people the loss of fear is a form of psychological rebirth. A woman who took the course in Hopkins, Minnesota, said that "it was like being let out of a cage." A Tallahassee, Florida, student described it as having helped him "break out of a neurotic pattern of living." A man attending a vocational institution in California used the unusual imagery of saying that before taking the course his life was "like a mirror covered with sticky scotch tape, but now the mirror is clear and shows all the wonderful things in life that I had missed before."

Many doctors and educators have attested to the

course's effectiveness in helping people. Dr. David Fink, a Los Angeles psychiatrist who took the course, wrote a book, *Be Your Real Self*, in which he stated:

Fortunately, fear of one's fellows, excessive self-consciousness, can be quickly and easily—I should add pleasantly—cured. I have seen thirty-five persons cured of excessive self-consciousness within sixteen (now fourteen) weeks. In that short time, they learned the techniques of getting along with other people. How did they do it? They took the Dale Carnegie Course in Human Relations.

If you are dissatisfied with your ability to get along with others, enroll in the Dale Carnegie Course . . . and if you are a teacher and you are satisfied with your ability to get along with others, take the course anyhow. The methods used in teaching this course today will become the methods of teaching all courses tomorrow.

Dr. James N. Holm, professor of speech and director of forensics at Kent State University, and a Dale Carnegie instructor for seventeen years, gave an evaluation of the course in an article which appeared in *Today's Speech* (September, 1960): "Students learn to say more nearly the right words in the right tones and at the right time because they have unconsciously been altering their attitudes and drives as they put the Carnegie rules into practice. It works."

Still another author, Vincent F. Sullivan, in *How to*

Sell Your Way into the Big Money, gave this illustration:

One evening in 1944, one of our salesmen, Clarence G. Klopp, delivered a beautiful presentation showing the effectiveness of our Color Comic advertising. He held his audience from beginning to end. The presentation was given to a large staff of salesmen sprinkled with sales executives. The audience was most liberal with its applause. Frankly, I was astounded because Klopp had been with us since 1931 and during the years, while his record for willingness had been good, he was noted for his inability to express himself freely, even before three or four persons. This lack . . . had been an anchor around his neck. A few days after his brilliant presentation, I met him for a few minutes and he explained that he had recently finished the speaking course given by Dale Carnegie.

I dismissed the matter from my mind. Some two months later, Klopp resigned his job to accept an advertising sales job with a magazine at almost double his salary.

Early in 1949, another situation developed where a friend of mine was promoted to the vice-presidency of a company at the age of 34. When I discovered that he attributed his promotion to the same sixteen-week Dale Carnegie course, I decided to investigate.

I got in touch with the local Dale Carnegie office and was advised that I could join one of their classes starting the following week. And that is how I entered into one of the most fascinating periods of my life.

The improvement that takes place in a person varies with the individual. In the stratospheric category is the story of Art Brown, a New Yorker who took the course to gain more self-confidence to help him in his work as an air conditioning salesman. After the session on enthusiasm, he burst into class the following week to recall how Frank Bettger, a Carnegie graduate, wrote a book on how he increased his income $20,000 a year by using the Dale Carnegie techniques. "Well," cried Brown, "Frank Bettger was a piker." He proceeded to tell how he had been so charged with enthusiasm that he sailed into the executive offices of a leading New York department store where he had always been rebuffed before and sold the buyer $565,000 worth of air conditioning equipment.

The story was taken with a grain of salt until a few weeks later, at a Carnegie demonstration meeting in the Hotel Roosevelt, when a prospective student was asked why he wanted to take the course. He introduced himself as a buyer for the department store, adding, "I want to find out how Art Brown sold me over a half million dollars' worth of air conditioning equipment."

In another stirring case, a former housing official in Massachusetts was unable to get a penny for housing from the state legislature. After going before that august body three times without success, he went to a member of the Dale Carnegie staff and explained his problem. A total of three Carnegie instructors spent a couple of weeks drilling the official in Carnegie techniques. The latter then went back before the legislature and won a $200 million appropriation.

Both of these incidents are unusual, but the underlying circumstances are not uncommon. Most people are satisfied with much more modest triumphs in their lives: a promotion, a raise, a sale they couldn't make previously, a friendly word from someone they thought disliked them—the stuff of which daily life is composed.

A Waldorf-Astoria maid reported exuberantly that she had learned from the course how to get along better with the other maids. A foreman at a metal plant in St. Paul, advised by his doctor to take the course for his nerves, rolled up his sleeves near the end of the course to show how he had gotten rid of a skin rash. A housewife in Newcastle, Pennsylvania, midway through the course said in a half-shy, half-embarrassed way that on the previous Monday morning she had found the courage to introduce herself to her next door neighbor after having lived in the neighborhood two years; previously, she said, she had purposely avoided any meeting for fear of what to say and talk about when they met, even going so far as to hang her Monday wash in her own basement to avoid a chance meeting. As a result of having introduced herself, she said she was invited in for coffee; she thoroughly enjoyed herself, confessed her shyness, and learned that her neighbor was similarly afflicted. She ended the talk by saying, "You don't know how wonderful it is to get invited to someone's home and find that you want to go."

To each of these people the change in their own feelings, which brought about the result they wanted, was a miracle. That word—miracle—is used repeatedly in connection with the course: "the miracle that happened to me . . ." "the miracles I've seen. . . ." Miracle is a strong word. It is an exaggeration. It is questionable if there are any miracles. If there were, one man's miracle might be another man's poison; what seems miraculous to one person may be commonplace to another, perhaps distasteful. For Art Brown, selling a half million dollars' worth of air conditioning equipment at one lick, after repeated failures, seemed like a miracle; to the Pennsylvania housewife who was so shy she hung her wash in the cellar to avoid having to speak to her neighbor, being able to say "hello" and to be invited into her neighbor's kitchen for coffee, and enjoying herself, seemed like a miracle. The person who suddenly feels that he has discovered what it means to be alive, to become aware of life and the little things that make up daily life—that too seems like a miracle. The stutterer or stammerer who notices improvement in his affliction, or becomes less self-conscious about it, feels that he has experienced a miracle. As these people respond to the blessing that has come to them, and see the beneficial effects in others who have similarly undergone a happy experience with equal meaning for them, the word miracle comes quickly to the lips.

There are probably as many reasons for taking the course as there are students. A Colorado man wanted to give the commencement address at his daughter's high school graduation. An Illinois man wanted to become superintendent of his Sunday school. A woman in Great Britain wanted to give speeches on pig breeding. A woman in Miami said she wanted to take the course for two reasons: one to improve her memory, and she couldn't remember the second reason. A New Yorker said he wanted to learn to cope with the "Hidden Persuaders." Many men want to gain business advantage—to present themselves and their ideas more effectively. Many would like to get along better with other people. Numerous students take the course on the recommendation of Carnegie graduates or students.

Several have been ordered to take it by their employers (usually for the human relations training) on pain of being fired.

People often take the course for a specific reason and then discover that they get something more valuable out of it than the thing they originally sought. The unexpected bonus usually is the ability to get along better with other people. A Dallas man started the course by coolly announcing that he didn't like people. "I don't care whether they live or die," he said, "but I do like money. I want just as much of it as I can get. I know that I must learn more about people in order to get them to part with their money. That's why I am here." At the final session the same student didn't disavow his liking for money, but he did say he had discovered that "people are nice and I enjoy being with them."

An article in *Look* magazine (May 25, 1948) observed:

It is the fashion in sophisticated quarters to scoff at Carnegie. But psychologist Henry C. Link believes that the very fact that the Carnegie philosophy "describes simple and obvious techniques of friendship makes it important because our civilization has so thoroughly ignored these values. Moreover, though these techniques may be simple in theory, they are not easy in practice. And though their purpose may seem selfish, their effort is to create habits of unselfishness. Mr. Carnegie's message may not be academically intellectual, but it is profound. The winning of friends is truly the deepest concern of the world today. Neither peace nor prosperity can come except through more universal friendship and better personalities."

The Carnegie people insist that they have neither the desire nor the ability to "change" a personality, in spite of the sometimes startling improvements that occur as a result of the training. Dorothy Carnegie, widow of Dale Carnegie, who now owns and operates the organization of Dale Carnegie & Associates, Inc., explains it this way: "We can't change a personality—and we wouldn't if we could. All we try to do is to help a person use more effectively whatever abilities and natural assets he has. By throwing off the constrictions of fear, a person is able to express whatever he is freely, and to reveal his personality in such a way as to fulfill himself. The joy and power of this new freedom of self-expression often changes a person's way of living, thinking, and acting, but he himself is not 'changed'—he is merely using his own resources to a greater extent than ever before. We cannot give him any quality he does not already possess within himself. But we can make him aware of his own qualities and inspire him to use them."

Harry O. Hamm, the Dale Carnegie representative in southern California, expresses it this way: "The course won't give people intelligence they don't have. If a person comes in 'an ignoramus,' he will go out an ignoramus, but he should be a more effective ignoramus. You can't give anyone intelligence they don't have. But whatever intelligence they do possess can be released to make them as effective as possible."

Mr. Hamm could have had in mind the occasional student who is transformed by the course from a shrinking violet into a raging extrovert. Dale Carnegie used to cringe when he recalled a misguided student who, when asked what he got out of the course, struck a dramatic pose, thrust his index finger into the air, and cried: "Seven hundred and forty-two dollars, a new confidence, a new courage, and thirty-nine new friends."

Because of the wide variation in results, Carnegie used to forewarn his students against discouragement by urging them not to measure their progress against that of other people in the class but to "compare yourself only with yourself . . . measure yourself now against what you were when you enrolled in the course."

This advice is given repeatedly during the Dale Carnegie Course, which has become an important part of the booming adult education movement in the United States. Some educators feel that the revolutionary teaching methods eventually will become a standardized part of most school curriculums, but others still resist them because they aren't academic enough. The Carnegie method is based on one fundamental principle: Does it work? If a technique is effective in bringing about the desired result, it is adopted; if not, it is dropped.

There is no doubt that some of the technique is what the sophisticated call "corn"—and undoubtedly it lends itself to ridicule. Some people resist the whole Carnegie approach because they feel that perhaps they are being taken in. A remarkable thing is that when even the most skeptical apply this particular brand of "Carnegie corn," they usually discover, to their amazement, that it works. As one bemused student from the higher intellectual reaches said, "I came to scoff and stayed to marvel."

Experience has shown that how much a person gets out of the course always depends on what he puts into it. Carnegie people say that anyone with normal intelligence, the ability to learn and a desire to benefit, should make progress in some degree if he is willing to work at applying what he learns. Dale Carnegie held that anyone who got only his money's worth was cheated.

"You should get a thousand times more than what you paid for it in lifelong benefits," he said.

This may be overstating the case, but the dedication and zeal of the students, graduates, and instructors is proof of the basic truth of what he said. People often travel prodigious distances, sometimes under extreme hardship, to take or give the training, and their testimonials ring with sincerity and gratitude. Further proof of the course's effectiveness is that some five hundred major companies—including General Motors —have made the course part of their executive-training program.

The Dale Carnegie Course in Effective Speaking and Human Relations, as it's formally known, currently is offered in more than 1,200 localities in the United States and Canada and in 35 foreign countries, costing from $135 to $185, depending on the locality in which it's given. In addition to the Dale Carnegie Course, Dale Carnegie & Associates, Inc. also offers the Dorothy Carnegie Course in Personal Development for Women, originated by Dorothy Carnegie, who succeeded her husband as president of the company; and the Dale Carnegie Sales Course for men and women actively engaged in selling.

The Carnegie course has been given in many unusual places, including a Navajo Indian reservation,

Wall Street, the Harvard Club, numerous prisons, the New York Institute for the Blind, in various service clubs, the United States Coast Guard, a Hollywood motion picture studio, and to carefully screened patients in mental institutions.

In an even more unusual setting, according to *Collier's* magazine (January 15, 1949), "Two missionaries from Africa, although they have not held formal classes in the jungle . . . reported to Carnegie that they successfully applied the salient principles of the course to a group of frustrated savages, a feat which Carnegie shrugs off as simply more evidence that both the disease and cure are universal."

Since the course was first offered in 1912, about one million persons have completed the training, ranging from a 10-year-old Wisconsin girl and a 12 year old boy, to an 83-year-old man. Their ranks have included executives, laborers, doctors, lawyers, engineers, actors, students, housewives, career women, socialites, financiers, teachers, bankers, pilots, policemen, clergymen, and others. Harry O. Humm, the southern California representative, recently said that his classes had included everything except a steeplejack—and in the next class there was a steeplejack.

A curious facet of the course is the strange mingling of the various worlds the students come from. A laborer may sit with openmouthed wonder as he hears a socialite relate the thorny problems connected with a debutante ball; and she may be equally astounded to learn of a world where people worry about how to pay the gas bill and whether to risk being fired by asking for a raise. These people may never again speak to one another after the course ends, but during the fourteen weeks they attend class together, their lives are incredibly welded and interwoven as they pursue a common goal and help one another try to realize the best that is in each of them.

The Carnegie officials themselves feel that despite the encouraging statistical increase in the number of persons taking the training, they can realize their own potential only when the public comes to understand correctly what the course is about. This educational face lifting is loftily referred to as "upgrading the image" that was created in the public mind following publication of *How to Win Friends and Influence People*. Carnegie executives note that in former days the general public often erroneously assumed that anyone who took the course had something wrong with him, but now it is becoming more widely accepted that people who take the course generally are "success-minded —in search of the plus skills that will help them get ahead faster in a highly competitive society."

A Carnegie executive noted recently that today almost no one takes the course under an assumed name, and fewer people reverse the dust jacket on their copy of *How to Win Friends and Influence People* so others can't see what they're reading. "Just the other day I saw a man reading the book on the subway, holding it up so anybody could see the title," he said. "I knew then that we had come a long way."

2.
THE MAN WHO
DID IT

**A Kind of
Horatio Alger
Story**

OUT OF THE dreams, disappointments, frustrations, and needs of his own life, Dale Carnegie was inspired to found the course that today bears his name. In a foreword to *How to Win Friends and Influence People*, Lowell Thomas, one-time associate of Carnegie's, relates the highlights of Carnegie's youth and early manhood. He tells about the grinding poverty of the

Missouri farm where Carnegie spent his boyhood, Carnegie's struggle for education and the searing humiliation of being the poorest boy in the college, his despair at not making a name for himself in athletics and his subsequent triumphs in public speaking, the years he spent on the road as a salesman—first for a correspondence school (he once sold a course to a lineman working atop a pole) and later for a packing house—and finally his ill-fated efforts to become an actor in New York and to sell trucks there.

Discouraged, broke, and at loose ends, Carnegie in 1912 took counsel with himself and reached a decision that was to be a milestone in his life and the lives of thousands of others:

"Since I had spent four years studying in the State Teachers College at Warrensburg, Missouri, preparing to teach, I would make my living teaching adult classes in night schools. Then I would have my days free to read books, prepare lectures, write novels and short stories. I wanted 'to live to write and write to live.'

"What subjects should I teach at night? As I looked back and evaluated my own college training, I saw that the training and experience I had had in public speaking had been of more practical value to me in business —and in life—than everything else I had studied in college all put together. Why? Because it had wiped out my timidity and lack of self-confidence and given me the courage and assurance to deal with people. It had also made clear that leadership usually gravitates to the man who can get up and say what he thinks.

"I applied for a position teaching public speaking in the night extension courses both at Columbia University and New York University, but these universities decided they could struggle along somehow without my help."

Carnegie, then 24, went to the Young Men's Christian Association on 125th Street with the idea of teaching a course there in public speaking. The manager was unimpressed but invited him to come to a "social evening" the coming Tuesday "and if you want to make a speech or do a stunt, come along and you're welcome."

Carnegie went and, to piano accompaniment, recited James Whitcomb Riley's "Knee Deep in June," and "Giddyap Napoleon, It Looks like Rain." He hadn't lost the touch that had made him the toast of Warrensburg, and the manager agreed to let him give classes in public speaking. But as Carnegie later told the story:

"The Y had so little faith in my public speaking course that it refused to risk $2 a night—a teacher's salary in those days. So I said, 'I will work on a profit-sharing basis. From the first money that comes in, you pay for your printed matter and postage. If there is any profit we can divide it any way you like.'

". . . I had to show concrete results and show them quickly. What a challenge that was! These adults didn't come to my classes because they wanted college credit or social prestige. They came for one reason only: they wanted to solve their problems. They wanted to be able to stand up on their feet and say a few words at a business meeting without fainting from fright. Salesmen wanted to be able to call on a tough customer without having to walk around the block three times to get up courage. They wanted to develop poise and self-confidence. They wanted to get ahead in business. They wanted to have more money for their families. And since they were paying their tuition on an installment basis—and they stopped paying if they didn't get results—and since I was being paid, not a salary, but a percentage of the profits, I had to be practical if I wanted to eat."

The first session Carnegie taught in the YMCA was a milestone. He began teaching public speaking as he had been taught—by lecturing. But to his dismay he discovered that after thirty minutes he had told everything he knew, and he had an hour and a half to fill up. In desperation—and in a moment of inspiration—he had the students stand and talk about themselves and their problems. "Without knowing what I was doing," he later said, "I stumbled on the best method of conquering fear."

Within a few months Carnegie was teaching classes nightly in YMCAs in New York, Philadelphia, Baltimore, and Wilmington, and making $30 to $40 a night commission. By 1914 his weekly income had reached $400 and he rented an office in Times Square, hired instructors, and wrote pamphlets to standardize his methods. He also found time to take a short-story-writing course at New York University and attend the Columbia School of Journalism and the Baltimore School of Commerce and Finance.

Soon Carnegie was selling articles to magazines, while continuing to teach his classes. He also won considerable notice by giving some lectures at Carnegie Hall.

In 1916 Carnegie was in his office when he got a phone call from Lowell Thomas. Thomas, then an instructor in the English department at Princeton, had been asked to speak at the Smithsonian Institution in Washington. He had seen Carnegie's name posted outside Carnegie Hall as a teacher of public speaking and wanted to offer his speech for criticism. Carnegie listened to the speech, complimented Thomas on it, suggested a few minor changes which Thomas thought were excellent, and the two took an instant liking to one another.

Three years later—after Carnegie had spent eighteen months in Camp Upton, Long Island, during World War I—Thomas proposed to make a world tour with his war films of Allenby in Jerusalem and Lawrence in Arabia. His London season was a sensation. After that he asked Carnegie to act as his manager. Thomas himself couldn't put on his Allenby-Lawrence production at enough places at once, so he sent Dale Carnegie on tour with two other road companies, traveling through Great Britain, the United States, and Canada. The two men remained lifelong friends. In fact, Lowell Thomas regarded Dale Carnegie as some sort of phenomenon—a genius in his field.

After the tour, Carnegie returned to New York to resume his classes. At that time, 1922, he left the YMCA and went in business for himself, giving his own classes.

Meanwhile, Carnegie had married Lolita Baucaire, a French-German woman whom he had met in Europe in 1921. The marriage ended in divorce after a decade. It was during this period that Carnegie began writing books. His favorite was *Lincoln, the Unknown*.

Carnegie's other books included: *Public Speaking, a Practical Course for Business Men* (1926), the original standard text for his public speaking classes, revised in 1931 to *Public Speaking and Influencing Men in Business; Little Known Facts About Well Known People* (1943); *Five Minute Biographies* (1937); the fabulously successful *How to Win Friends* (1936); *Biographical Roundup* (1945); and *How to Stop Worrying and Start Living* (1948). About the last-named, a *New York Times* book review described it as Carnegie's "latest blueprint for a social Garden of Eden . . . so choked with formula and exhortation and case histories" that no reader could be "entirely unrewarded." Although the book didn't have the appeal of *How to Win Friends,* which one critic called "a combination of great names and simple truths," it sold over one hundred thousand copies, a phenomenally good sale by publishers' standards.

Carnegie also wrote one novel, "The Blizzard," which was never published. Critics who saw the manuscript described it as one of the worst books ever written. Carnegie himself agreed and added that it was unfortunate that "The Blizzard" wasn't published as a monumental example of how not to write fiction.

With the success that accompanied his various activities, Carnegie bought a comfortable home on Long Island, in Forest Hills, Queens, a borough of New York City, and furnished it with antiques he had acquired in his travels. His pride was a chair in his bedroom that had belonged to his idol, Abraham Lincoln, and a Napoleonic bed.

He loved birds and squirrels and was proud because a squirrel would come into his bedroom study and feed from his desk. He also loved to take his Boston bulldog, Rex, for walks, and he greatly admired a set of dinosaur tracks he bought from Yale's Peabody Museum and had implanted in concrete in his back yard.

But his greatest pride was his garden. He would occasionally pause and look about him in wonder. "It's incredible to me that I could live in a comfortable house like this," he once remarked to his wife Dorothy, whom he had married in 1944. "I just wish I could have known in the days when I was so poor that I would have a garden, be able to travel, and own antiques."

He rarely smoked or drank; he attended church infrequently but had a weakness for ministers—probably due to his strict Methodist upbringing and his mother's deep involvement with the church—and he often gave his course to ministers without charge. (Dorothy Carnegie has not perpetuated this policy on grounds that "it discriminates against other worthy classes and professions.")

Like most successful men, Carnegie was devoted to

his work. He thought of little else every waking hour of the day; even when he took walks in the woods he would talk shop; he worked days, nights, holidays, and expected his staff to share his enthusiasm.

Carnegie dwelt in a shadowland between the arts and business, but he was not known as a good businessman. Despite a lively sense of thrift, he let no expense stand in the way of improving his course; for it he wanted only the best. He was more interested in helping his students than in making money out of them, according to his associates. One colleague recalled that Carnegie kept loose records of payments and rarely looked at them; he almost never sent a bill to a student who failed to meet his payments, it was said. Once he turned down a lucrative offer from a cigarette company that wanted to sponsor his course on the radio because he wouldn't permit it to be exploited for entertainment purposes. Carnegie was so wrapped up in his work that he was often oblivious of almost everything else in life.

The concentrated energy and dedication he gave to his job had much to do with his success, but there was another and more important factor: the particular genius of Carnegie the teacher, the speech expert.

Carnegie, above all, was a pragmatist. The only question he concerned himself with was: Does it work? If it worked, he would adopt it for his course; if it didn't work, he wanted no part of it. Ormond Drake, Associate Dean at New York University, an eminent speech authority and a former Carnegie instructor, said Carnegie believed that if, as a result of taking the course, "your income didn't go up, if you didn't become happier by becoming more effective in speech, if you didn't sell more products, if you couldn't convince others of the rightness of the thing you espoused, then the course was worthless."

Carnegie had little patience with theory or abstract thought. He wanted only the practical, the useful, the functional. But coupled with his pragmatism was an incredible ability to learn from everything in life. Ormond Drake said, "He was a fantastic observer. He could capitalize on practical experience better than anyone I ever knew. He was always writing things down and asking questions. He was terribly dogmatic about some things but his mind was not closed.

"He could not only observe but could capitalize on his observations. I used to be amazed how he could see some thing happen and six months later he came out in print with it. I myself didn't see it right or I didn't see its application to people. That was the heart of Dale Carnegie's genius—to be able to capitalize on experience.

"Over and over I saw this happen. He would go visit

someone, and there's another chapter; watch his dog, and there's another. Once at an NBC radio studio we judged a speaking contest. To me it was just another contest and soon forgotten. To Dale it was an experience for his filing card cabinet. Months later I heard him deliver a speech in the Murray Hill Hotel. By this time that studio experience had become a five- or six-minute talk; he called it 'A Chunk of Life.' Everything had a lesson for Dale."

At another time Drake said about him: "He was a happy man. One of the most honest persons I ever knew. When I met him I wondered if he was trying to clean up and get out. But I learned that he believed everything he said 100 per cent. He had no qualms about standing before an organization like the Economic Club and offering the truth of his teaching as firmly as if he were talking to six ladies at a private gathering."

Carnegie once was invited to address the Dutch Treat Club in New York. A member of his staff advised him not to accept, pointing out that it was made up of editors, publishers, and advertising men. "They're the toughest bunch in America," he said. "They'll eat you alive."

"If you've got truth and honesty on your side, you've got a good shield and buckler," Carnegie replied.

This conversation took place just after publication of *How to Win Friends,* and Carnegie was the target of mass abuse and ridicule. He accepted the invitation and went to the luncheon; when it came time to speak he rose and said simply:

"I know there's considerable criticism of my book. People say I'm not profound and there's nothing in it new to psychology and human relations. This is true. Gentlemen, I've never claimed to have a new idea. Of course I deal with the obvious. I present, reiterate, and glorify the obvious—because the obvious is what people need to be told. The greatest need of people is to know how to deal with other people. This should come naturally to them, but it doesn't.

"I am told that you are a hostile audience. But I plead 'not guilty.' The ideas I stand for are not mine. I borrowed them from Socrates, I swiped them from Chesterfield, I stole them from Jesus. And I put them in a book. If you don't like their rules, whose would you use? I'll be glad to listen."

He received a thunderous standing ovation. Then he made use of the experience, putting it into his instructor's manual as one example of dealing with a hostile audience.

Carnegie had an intuitive feel for people that helped him tremendously in developing his course. Many speech experts who watched him work describe him as a great teacher. He was able to bring out qualities in his students as few other instructors could, often throwing himself into the effort so thoroughly that he and the student would emerge exhausted but usually triumphant.

Carnegie's philosophy of teaching was that an effective speech doesn't come from the outside in. "You don't superimpose a set of gestures and beautiful words like a suit of fine clothes onto your heart and mind. Rather, you get an idea from your mind and a heart full of feeling, and let it go. A good speech flows from the inside out, and nothing can stop you from being a good speaker if you're an intelligent human being."

Several Carnegie associates commented on his outstanding ability to draw people out through questions. Mrs. Ann McClelland, who has worked closely with her husband, Dr. Stewart McClelland, a Carnegie official, said, "He almost literally could put his hand down a man's throat and pull his heart out of him. Nobody else could do it. He knew how to ask just the right questions at the right time."

It is often mistakenly believed that Carnegie was an unknown who sprang into prominence with the publication of *How to Win Friends and Influence People.*

National and international fame did follow the book, but he had already established a sound reputation wherever the classes were given and had made a name for himself with his writing, teaching, lecturing, and various broadcasting enterprises. As his course expanded, he wrote pamphlets as teaching aids to illustrate the human relations principles; these pamphlets later were to serve as the nucleus of *How to Win Friends*.

Carnegie also conducted a popular radio program, "Little Known Facts About Well Known People," on a New York radio station, and he wrote several articles for the *Reader's Digest* and other publications. In 1937 he conducted a barnstorming tour around the country, holding a five-night school on human relations and salesmanship, with Richard Borden, a New York University professor and noted speech authority, and later with Frank Bettger, whose fabulous insurance sales had enabled him to retire at age 42, after only thirteen years in the business. During and after World War II, Carnegie often conducted these five-night clinics throughout the United States without assistance from others. Many people who attended these sales clinics mistakenly thought they were the regular Dale Carnegie Course.

After the publication of *How to Win Friends,* which at the peak of its popularity sold five thousand copies a day, month after month, Carnegie went to Europe; he left his aides to run the business, then known as The Carnegie Institute of Effective Speaking and Human Relations, founded in 1933.

While Carnegie was in Europe traveling and writing, his business was falling apart at home. The depression and the lack of his direct supervision took their toll. The business had grown from a one-room office to two floors and a penthouse in a building in mid-town Manhattan. Suddenly, in 1939, Carnegie began to receive frantic S O S's for money to meet the bills. He rushed home and over a period of a month dismissed the entire staff of thirty-five people, closed the Manhattan office, and moved it to his own home in Forest Hills. He was ready to start over again, undismayed by the misfortune, advancing money from his pocket to keep the courses going until the bills were paid and efficient management could recoup the losses.

A few years later, in 1944, the Dale Carnegie Course took on a true national coloring for the first time. It had been offered by various business schools throughout the country, but subsequently it spread beyond these narrow confines. The previous year Carnegie had incorporated under the name Dale Carnegie Courses, Inc. On October 1, 1944, a partnership was formed to conduct the licensing business under which territories outside the New York area were franchised to "sponsors." (Sponsors are the individuals licensed to present and operate the Dale Carnegie Course in a given area.) The setup called for the various sponsors to be in charge of their areas, responsible to Carnegie. In 1945, Carnegie laid the foundation for the present parent organization, Dale Carnegie & Associates, Inc., a private stock company, with himself as president and his wife Dorothy as vice-president.

Carnegie and Dorothy Price Vanderpool were married in 1944, after a romance that began in her native Tulsa. She had taken the course and was a personal friend of the Tulsa sponsor, H. Everett Pope.

Dorothy and her mother heard Carnegie speak in Tulsa, and afterwards they joined Pope and Carnegie for coffee. Dorothy recalls that she liked Carnegie at once and he seemed to like her. After the women left, Carnegie, who had been a bachelor for thirteen years, expressed a lively interest in Dorothy by questioning Pope about her.

Following Carnegie's Tulsa visit, he sent Dorothy several letters. "They were not romantic exactly," she says, "but they were a little warmer than business letters." In October, 1943, he offered her a job in his New York office as his secretary. Dorothy accepted and came to New York after the first of the year.

After a somewhat tempestuous courtship, in which Dorothy once quit her job after a spat with Carnegie and started to pack and go home, only to have him turn on the how-to-win-friends charm and influence her into staying, they were married November 5, 1944.

Dorothy, who is five-feet-nine, slender and with reddish-brown hair and green eyes, took an interest in Carnegie's work from the start. But she didn't become actively involved until they took a vacation in the Canadian Rockies and boredom drove her to authorship.

"It started like WPA work," she recalls. "My husband got me started to keep me busy. We had been to the Canadian Rockies three or four times previously; he liked to hike over the trails or sit and admire the scenery. I got tired of this outdoor life. At night, when I wanted to dance, he wanted to go to bed early so he could get up at dawn and look at more scenery. I could ride those trails on horseback in my sleep. Finally he came up with a plan to keep me happy: 'Why don't you write a course for women?' he asked. I agreed and started right to work." That led to what is now known as the Dorothy Carnegie Course in Personal Development for Women.

In 1953, Mrs. Carnegie wrote a book, *How to Help Your Husband Get Ahead in his Social and Business Life.* The Chicago *Sunday Tribune,* reviewing the book, stated that the author had prescribed a pattern for wives to get along with their husbands, and "help them win friends and influence people." Subsequently it was published in some twenty languages. Later, Mrs. Carnegie wrote a second book, *Don't Grow Old— Grow Up* (1958).

Along with her writing and supervision of the Dorothy Carnegie Course, Mrs. Carnegie gave birth to a child, Donna Dale, in 1951—when Carnegie was 65. Carnegie was delighted by his first offspring and announced the event to newspapermen while on a trip in Italy. Mrs. Carnegie, who had remained behind in Forest Hills because of the forthcoming birth, had kept her pregnancy quiet and was somewhat piqued to find it announced to the world over the wire services.

It was only a few years later that Carnegie began to fail physically. For several months he had not been feeling well and he was especially disturbed by his inability to remember things. Subsequently it was discovered that he was suffering from hardening of the arteries, and a series of small strokes was interfering with his retentive powers. On several occasions he would start somewhere and find that he couldn't remember his destination. He began to rely more heavily on notes when he spoke, but could summon enough of the old magic to carry off speaking engagements with valor.

In 1954 he was happy when his old alma mater, Warrensburg State Teachers College, notified him that it was conferring on him an honorary degree; as one colleague said, he couldn't have been more pleased had it come from Harvard or Oxford. For two weeks he worked on his speech but discovered he couldn't remember it. This was to be one of the big occasions of his life, and it was a terrible blow to the man who had taught thousands how to think on their feet that he had to wind up reading one of the most important speeches he ever gave.

Despite his disability, the talk went well. *Newsweek* commented: "He spoke with his usual firmness (and enthusiasm), in an accent still of the Midwest. His natural body gestures were well timed, and his persuasive content was high. No doubt only the dignity of the occasion restrained his listeners from encouraging shouts of 'Atta boy!'"

A short time later Carnegie came down with an attack of shingles and made a slow recovery. For the first time the enthusiasm and bounce that characterized him was missing. He and Dorothy went to Bermuda for a vacation, taking along three-year-old Donna Dale. But the trip did Carnegie no good. He had to be brought back to the states and taken to a hospital. He gradually grew weaker. When it was obvious that he was dying, Mrs. Carnegie had him moved to the Forest Hills home where he wanted to be. For nine days Carnegie fought desperately for life, but finally, on a Wednesday morning, November 1, 1955, he slipped quietly into the great void of death; he would have been 67 years old on November 24.

Messages and bouquets poured in from all over the world from friends, admirers, and people who knew about him only through his work. Services were held in the Church-in-the-Gardens in Forest Hills. Services were also held in Missouri and, as he had requested, he was buried in Belton, near his parents. His obituary in the *New York Times* was a full column long and observed that he had been born in poverty and obscurity but found that a silver tongue could be more useful than a silver spoon in winning wealth and fame. The article also stated that "Mr. Carnegie's advice for successful living might be summed up in two of his maxims: 'Forget yourself; do things for others,' and 'Co-operate with the inevitable.' "

A modest monument designates Carnegie's grave, but his real memorial is the revolutionary teaching method he evolved through his courses.

3.
RELEASED
TO

ONE OF THE showcase graduates of the Dale Carnegie Course is Joe Foss, a World War II Marine captain who was the leading American ace in the Pacific theater of war; he is credited with having shot down twenty-six Zeros, "not counting smokers or probables." For his valor he holds the Congressional Medal of Honor; but before taking the Carnegie course, Foss said, "I'd

BE A PERSON

His Teaching on Practical Ways to Overcome Fear

rather have faced twenty-six Jap planes all at the same time than a room full of people." After taking the course, Foss became governor of the state of North Dakota and subsequently commissioner of the American Football League.

Fear is a dominant theme among people who sign up for the Dale Carnegie Course. It ranges in intensity and effect, but most people who enroll for the training admit to some degree of fear or discomfort when standing in front of a group of people to address them.

This varies from the person whose mind tightens up so he can't think easily on his feet to the Baltimore man who toppled over in a faint. In the latter case, Carnegie, who was teaching the class, bounded to the prostrate student's side and cried, "Within a month this man will be speaking from the stage with confidence"—a prediction that came to pass.

People react to fear in various ways, some of them humorous, some pathetic. Joe Reekton drove to a course demonstration session in Akron with his friend, Al Hutler; when Reekton stood to introduce himself he was so unnerved that he said, "My name is Al Hutler." A Louisville insurance executive boasted at the organization meeting that he did not need the course but would join to be with his friends; at the first session he forgot where he lived and also his wife's and children's names. The president of a Chicago radio and television corporation recalled that when he was sales manager of the company he attended a banquet of the National Association of Radio Manufacturers; he was seated at the head table; when told that he would be called on to say a few words, he slipped out of a side door and didn't return.

A New Mexico man went to a demonstration and forgot his own name; when laughter rippled through the room he leaped up to his full height of six-feet-six-inches to proclaim, "Maybe I can't remember my name, but I can lick any . . . in this room"—a declaration that went unchallenged. Still another man admitted to having been so frightened before taking the course that he wouldn't wear a hat or blow a horn at New Year's Eve parties. Harold Abbott, sponsor of the course in Kansas City, said that before he took the course "I couldn't stand up and second the motion." A Louisville student said that he wouldn't "lead my church group in 'silent prayer.' "

Others have reported less severe symptoms when the spotlight of public attention was focused on them: the mouth going dry, inability to talk, trembling voice, butterflies in the stomach, the shakes, knees pounding together; some have wept, giggled without control or even had hysterics. Despite the variation of the symptoms and their intensity, all the victims of these assorted symptoms had the same basic ailment—fear.

Early in his career Carnegie discovered that the biggest obstacle he had to overcome in teaching people public speaking was to help them conquer their fear. Telling them not to be afraid did no good. Neither did it help to remind them that there was nothing to be afraid of, or that they were being foolish. To the victims of fear it is a very real and terrible thing, and it won't disappear by rational reasoning because it has no rational basis to begin with.

Through his unique pragmatic approach Carnegie hit upon a practical way to overcome fear, and, as usual, he found a quotation to back him up—Emerson's immortal advice that is quoted repeatedly throughout the Carnegie course: "Do the thing you fear to do and the death of fear is certain."

Carnegie discovered this truth at his first class in the 125th Street YMCA when, through desperation, he had his students stand and talk to kill time. He immediately recognized the validity of the adage that the best way to learn is not to be told what to do but to learn to do by doing—to learn to speak by speaking. But due to his keen sense of observation, he also sensed that he had hit on something important and effective. It will be recalled that he later said, "Without knowing what I was doing, I stumbled on the best method of conquering fear."

To understand how revolutionary his discovery was, it is necessary to note how public speaking was taught up to that time—and still is—in many schools and colleges. The accepted method was to teach by lecturing, just as Carnegie had been taught. Instructors concentrated more on the theory of speech than its practice. Seated behind a desk, they told how to plant one foot firmly to the rear and throw the weight on the ball of the forward foot; how to gesture with full arm, middle arm, and the hand; how to project the voice, to pronounce clearly, the proper way to breathe. For several months the student was lectured on the traditional methods of declamation, and finally he was unleashed to solo with a five-minute speech; then he was seated and tested on his knowledge of the theory of speaking, given a mark, and sent forth as a polished public speaker—at least theoretically.

Carnegie not only had his students start talking at the opening bell, but had them keep talking at each class session, paying little or no attention to most of the traditional elements that made up academic speech courses. He discovered by observation—through his genius for recognizing the obvious—that if a person knew what he was talking about (had "earned the right" to talk about it) and was enthusiastic about it ("an eager desire to impart knowledge into the minds of others"), the gestures and delivery would largely take care of themselves. He wasn't concerned about stance, breathing, formalized gestures, or any of the other traditional concepts, as long as the speaker was natural.

"We're teaching people to give an acceptable talk," he said, "not to become orators."

In his handbook for instructors, Carnegie stated:

I beg of instructors not to think of this as a public speaking course. Think of it as a course in destroying fear and building self-confidence. Think of it as a course in human relations. Think of it as a new way of life. For it often is just that. When a man banishes fear and develops confidence, his ceilings will become higher and his visibility unlimited. . . .

Fear causes more physical illness than germs. Jesus condemned fear more than he condemned sin. Fear is probably the greatest of all sins. It is a sin against the abundant life we should be living. It is a sin against our health. Above all else, it is a sin against our children, for if they are brought up by fearful, shy, self-doubting parents, they are almost sure to go through life only half living because of timidity. . . . Above all else, we are developing skills in acquiring courage.

The Carnegie approach naturally outraged many college speech teachers because it violated practically everything they had been taught and were passing along. They denounced Carnegie as a charlatan and a fraud, protesting that his methods couldn't possibly work. However, some speech teachers and authorities on the subject recognized what Carnegie had to offer and supported him. Among them was William A. D.

Millson of John Carroll University; in an article in the highly respected *Quarterly Journal of Speech* (February, 1941) he stated:

Dale Carnegie methods are successful enough with students to present a challenge to those of us in the academic field who are content with other methods in teaching of speech. And it is a challenge directed at more than our course method; it suggests that we have too long neglected the opportunity through speech to strengthen and develop the emotional life and attitudes of our students. It suggests that in our concentration on speech skills, we may often have harmed many of our emotionally handicapped. We have been so concerned with the practical side of speech— so eager to develop technical skill or artistic expression, so occupied with significance and its possible meaning to the individual student in terms of social adaptation and emotional adjustment. Perhaps we have yet to discover that our students have emotions as well as brains, and voice and body.

Educational authorities in several places, including those in Clark County and Floyd County, Indiana; the state of Vermont Department of Education; the City Department of Education, Baltimore, Maryland; and Hamilton County, Tennessee, Board of Education, have approved the Dale Carnegie Course for teachers to take as one of the courses required for renewal of a teacher's certificate. Many college speech teachers have become Carnegie instructors, often on a part-time basis, and Carnegie techniques are gradually infiltrating college courses, although Carnegie instructors must sign an agreement not to teach any competitive course or use the methods in other classes.

Dean Ormond Drake of New York University pointed out that there is a great physical difference in teaching for a college and for Carnegie. A college teacher usually sits at a desk, he said. "But you don't teach for Dale Carnegie that way. You're in the middle aisle, slapping backs and encouraging them. A college professor teaching a normal load, who taught as hard and energetically in classes every day as you have to teach for Dale Carnegie, couldn't live through it, he'd be so exhausted."

Drake said the effectiveness of the Carnegie method of teaching speech was demonstrated by the number of college graduates "from some of the finest schools in America" who took the Dale Carnegie Course after they had taken public speaking in college for credit and found that it did them no good; the Carnegie course gave them what they wanted.

This is due largely to the second great departure Carnegie made from traditional methods of teaching speech—the form his criticism took. Here is the heart of the Carnegie method:

There is no criticism, as it is commonly understood, in the Carnegie course. The instructor's handbook states: "One of the characteristics of a superb Dale Carnegie instructor is that he agrees with Addison that 'a true critic ought to dwell rather upon excellencies than imperfections.' The superb instructor will, at times, tactfully and gently give 'suggestions for improvement' but he never criticizes. Never, never, never."

Dr. L. Gray Burdin, vice-president in charge of instruction and educational development for Dale Carnegie & Associates, and a former speech teacher at Butler University in Indianapolis, said, "Academic people always think this is impossible. They say, 'How can you train without criticizing?'

"We say, 'You can inspire.'

"Does this mean we don't correct? No! We do correct, but there is more than one way to do it. This is the root of the Dale Carnegie philosophy of teaching:

"We never criticize; we show you instead how you can become more effective. That is the secret of our success. We tell you how to be more effective *and then show you how*. We don't just tell you what's wrong, but *immediately* show you how to do better.

"We concentrate on the whole person, not just the one thing he may not be doing the best possible way.

We want no one to sit down with the feeling that he failed. For that reason we use praise and inspiration as our teaching tools."

In the Red Book, given to students as their course manual, Dale Carnegie explained why he had adopted this approach:

Certain ambitious or impatient class members feel that they should be told about their faults at once. I tried that system long ago and discarded it. I found by long experience that telling a nervous, excited individual, a man blinded by fear, that he didn't half open his mouth, that he couldn't be heard in the back of the room, that he said "jist," that he failed to make his point, that he had no example and lacked enthusiasm—I found that such criticism terrified him and did more harm than good.

In place of criticism, Carnegie instructors "comment," achieving the desirable effects of criticism without its abrasive, ego-bruising effects. The Red Book explains:

Your instructor will try to make every comment helpful, so please pay attention to all comments. You will learn not only from suggestions regarding your own talks, but quite as much from the suggestions made by the instructor on the talks of other members. You will thus learn how to avoid the faults of some members and how to acquire the good characteristics of others.

How thoroughly Carnegie understood the destructive effects of criticism was indicated in a passage from *How to Win Friends*. He wrote:

If you and I want to stir up a resentment tomorrow that may rankle across the decades and endure until death, just let us indulge in a little stinging criticism—no matter how certain we are that it is justified.

When dealing with people, let us remember we are not dealing with creatures of logic. We are dealing with creatures of emotion, creatures bristling with prejudices and motivated by pride and vanity.

And criticism is a dangerous spark—a spark that is liable to cause an explosion in the powder magazine of pride.

Although praise is the primary teaching tool that Carnegie used, he emphasized in the manual that "I want to make it perfectly clear that I do not advocate giving students all praise and no help. That would be stupid. What is even worse, it would be insincere. I favor this technique: first praise a speaker for something he did correctly, and then, if time permits, drill him for something he did incorrectly. And *keep on drilling him until he shows improvement*. Finally, praise him again sincerely." This mixture of praise, "criticism," and more praise is referred to among Carnegie officials as a "Carnegie sandwich."

In the instructor's handbook Carnegie stated his insistence on sincerity even more firmly: "Any instructor who is guilty of flattery and insincerity will be dismissed by his employer the day he is caught. *There is no place in this course for anything but unswerving integrity.*"

Fundamentally, the method is based on a simple truth: Most of us are raised in an atmosphere of disapproval. One of the first words we hear is "No!" From then on it is dinned relentlessly into our ears and conscience. It becomes a dominant chord in our being, expressed in a variety of ways. From birth to death we hear "No!"—No! No! No! Don't do this, don't do that, don't do the other thing. The word *NO* is our heritage and legacy; we learn it from our parents and pass it along to our children in an unending chain.

Most of us carry the psychic scars from the disapproval of other people. We have been told we are too fat, too thin, we aren't very bright, our clothes don't fit, we lack social graces. We are compared unfavorably with others; we have standards imposed on us with no thought of our individual capacities and limitations. People have told us uncomplimentary things said about us. If we aren't told directly that we lack charm or lovableness, many of us have been made to feel it. The girl short on appeal is left brooding alone in the corner at dances; the boy who is awkward or bashful can't get a date or is stood up. How many subconscious minds are seared from the ugly sound of derisive laughter?

The teaching process in schools may often seem negative. Conventional methods generally are based on telling people what they do wrong, emphasizing their mistakes and shortcomings. We are chastised or punished for our failures and trespasses; our small victories and successes generally go unrecognized. Many people grow up and almost never hear the sweet music of a compliment, treasuring the few that have come their way. How many of us are soul-starved for a few kind words of appreciation? Too many human beings have felt the lash of failure and scorn so often that they have lost their spirit, their joy of life, and have taken refuge in a world of daydreams.

This barrage of negative criticism is a cumulative battering of the ego. We gradually come to feel unworthy or insignificant. This may not be a conscious feeling and we may not be aware it exists; it is usually rooted deep in the subconscious, a nagging subliminal awareness that we really don't amount to much.

To protect our damaged egos, the psychologists tell us, we build various defenses so we can face the outside world. These defenses may take many forms. Some people become shy or retiring, others are hostile, bitter, or aggressive; some become exhibitionists or write off existence as a cosmic joke unworthy of being taken seriously. We are ingenious creatures in the art of self-preservation.

Behind all defense mechanisms is one thing: fear! The fear of exposing the true self, the self buried deep inside us which whispers that, for all our worldly triumphs, we really don't amount to much, the self that is afraid that the mask we present to the world will slip and others will see our inadequacies and shortcomings.

Few people who stand before a group of other people and find themselves terrified stop to wonder what they're afraid of; they don't ask themselves why they're afraid. They only know the shattering effects of fear: the dryness in the mouth, shakiness of the voice, pounding of the knees, the mind going blank, an unreasoning, tormenting, agonizing fear—which, in truth, is not fear of the people who stand before us but fear of ourselves, the fear of exposure.

The Carnegie method of teaching puts the individual in an atmosphere of approval. Under the balm of praise he relaxes his defenses and allows some of his genuine personality to come through the real self that has been hiding behind so many defenses and disguises and masks, and he finds that it is acceptable; he is not despised or hated for what he is. He also comes to understand that other people have problems similar to his;

he is not alone in a hostile world; he is comforted by learning that others also are afraid; they are just as he is. At the same time that he lowers his defenses, others in the class are lowering theirs, and he comes to understand the "oneness" of people, that other humans share similar feelings of inadequacy and fear.

As fear disappears, antagonisms toward other people begin to ease; psychologists know that most hatred is based on fear, and when people cease to be hostile toward others, they begin to feel differently toward themselves and their environment. As a person gains a new perspective, he often develops new attitudes, and gradually his entire personality begins to change. About half way through the course some people have said they feel "strange" or "uncomfortable." They usually aren't sure what is going on, but they know that something is taking place. Because of the strong bond that develops in a class, as its members work toward the common goal of making the most of themselves and helping each other do the same, they open up to one another, creating a chain reaction that encourages them to open up more and more, stripping away the armor that has shielded them from other people, as the process of self-exploration continues.

Dr. Richard Bickel, sponsor of classes in South Africa, said the psychological effect of the course is to "provide people with a microscope under which they may examine the meaning of their own lives as well as the lives of their fellow students. It gives them a yard-stick with which they can measure their own talents, achievements, goals, and ambitions. It leaves them in possession of a comprehensive code for better living, which serves to inspire them, motivate them, guide them, and help them to a fuller, richer, and more re-warding life."

As students work up their talks each week, they must mull over their experiences in life and what they meant to them. For many people this is something new; they have gone through life largely thinking what they were told to think, saying what they were taught to say, never examining their own attitudes and feelings. Some of these people, for the first time, become acutely aware of their real feelings toward various aspects of life; they discover themselves, as it were—what the psychologists call "coming in contact with the self."

"It is a process of self-exploration," according to Dr. Stewart McClelland, former president of Lincoln Memorial University, and now a trainer of instructors for Dale Carnegie & Associates, Inc. "The student gets to the point where he is not afraid to express his own opinion, good, bad, or indifferent. He finds in the group a place where he can be himself. He finds companionship and understanding and gets the spirit to be what he wants to be."

A Columbia University psychologist who took the course told Carnegie: "We humans are very largely what we conceive ourselves to be. You take your students by simple easy stages to a point where they no longer think of themselves as being afraid. They are changed human beings because their conception of themselves is changed." Carnegie said, "There is no magic about the method, but there is about the result."

As old feelings of repression and layers of inhibition are stripped away, the person often has an exhilarating feeling of being suddenly freed from an invisible bond. Some people have said they felt as if they were let out of a cage. This big moment is the first step forward— the reversal of the negative patterns that work against a person realizing himself and his potentiality as a human being. When he starts going forward, he discovers that forces whose existence he never previously suspected are working for him and he doesn't have to do it all for himself. But it is equally important for him to understand that he alone must put these forces into forward motion. No one else can do that for him.

Carnegie put it this way: "What you get out of this training will depend almost entirely upon what you put into it. This is true not only of this training, but also of all education and life. Dr. Lawrence Lowell, former president of Harvard University, said: 'There is only one thing that will train the human mind and that is the voluntary use of the mind by the man himself. You may aid him, you may guide him, you may suggest to him, and above all else you may inspire him; but the only thing worth having is that which he gets by his own exertions, and that which he gets is in direct proportion to what he puts into it.' "

Carnegie was fond of quoting still another of his idols, the great psychologist William James, who noted that most humans function at only 10 per cent of their capacity. Many people do not have James's dictum in mind when they come to Carnegie, but they do realize that they aren't functioning at their full capacity as human beings. They may not have a specific fear problem, but merely want to enjoy a fuller and happier life and to get as much out of living as they can. Carnegie held that if, as a result of taking the course, "you improved your capacity for living by only one per cent it would be a bargain."

This is probably the real value of the course for most people—a greater joy in being alive, a greater awareness, a sense of euphoria. There may be no great miracles, no startling salary increases, no heroic job promotion, no world-shaking change in status or prestige. But instead, a new attitude, a better opinion of self and a more generous feeling toward others; they are no longer at war with the world, no longer feel the need to prove themselves.

When one achieves self-confidence, however, it gives the courage to tackle obstacles, and as a result startling things can and often do happen. These things may not necessarily be a direct result of the training, but a by-product of the person's new attitude. An example of what the Carnegie course, at its best, can do is the story of Maud Danziger of Cape Town, South Africa, as told by her sponsor, Robert E. Hopkins:

"Maud was a housewife who had built such a stout wall between herself and the outside world that for the last five years she had never voluntarily moved out of her house, not even to buy vegetables from the lorry which stopped outside her garden gate. The household shopping which she could not do by telephone her husband had to do for her. On one occasion when painters were at work on the outside of her house she let them do the whole place over in the wrong color rather than go out and speak to them.

"One evening her husband managed to persuade her to attend a Dale Carnegie demonstration meeting, where she won a $20 door prize. She was called three times before her husband could maneuver her into the aisle to receive it. When at last she came onto the stage she was one of the most frightened-looking people I had seen in all my experience.

"Maud started the course on Tuesday, June 4, 1957. She was so terribly nervous that when she got home, after the first two sessions, she lay awake all night shaking uncontrollably. By the third session she realized that this course was the most exciting and exhilarating thing that had happened to her for very many years. It lifted her completely out of the narrow world she had shaped for herself and suddenly life became a challenge.

"After finishing her course Maud was trained and worked as a graduate assistant. She approached the South African Broadcasting Corporation and was engaged to make a series of three broadcasts in their 'Woman's Hour,' where she told her story. She called it 'The Miracle.' She has since broadcast another series entitled 'Adventure in Adult Living,' which is based on the teachings of the Dorothy Carnegie Course, and she has also given these talks to many women's associations in Cape Town.

"She started working as a secretary, and at the same time was trained and qualified as an instructor for the Dorothy Carnegie Course. She took the Sales Course and won the Sales Course Championship Award. For nearly a year she sold the Dale Carnegie Course for me, and eventually she became my personal secretary. In three years this same woman, who for so long had been incapable of accepting the smallest responsibility, had contributed $6,000 toward the family income. She has just returned from a seven-month tour of England and the Continent with her daughter, thus realizing her first major goal in life since taking the course."

A fitting postscript to the story of Maud Danziger might be a message from Carnegie to his instructors:

"Unless you have been teaching this course for years, you can't possibly appreciate the almost incredible effects you, as the instructor, can have on the lives and personalities of your class members. With the right kind of teaching, you not only help them increase their income and their popularity, but you also help them to conquer fear, banish worry, improve their health, increase their happiness, and transform their personalities. Fear defeats more people than any other one thing in the world."

Once fear is defeated, the student is ready to undertake the next phase in building his new personality—the mellowing process of improving his human relations.

4.

The Dale Carnegie Emphasis

DISCOVERING

**on the Place of
Human Relations in Life**

OTHER PEOPLE

OLIVER K. WHITING, who holds the franchise for Great
Britain, recently tried to enroll a British industrialist
in the course in hopes that he would have his employees also take the training. The industrialist, a
formidable figure in the John Bull tradition, briskly
said, "Look here, Whiting, I make some three hundred speeches a year, you know, and you can't tell me
anything about making speeches."

Whiting pointed out that in the United States industry had found that the course aided in communication between people. The Britisher scoffed. Whiting replied, "Let me give you an example. You sit here behind your polished desk, the head of this great firm. You decide you want to see one of your employees tomorrow; the chances are that he will be so scared that he won't sleep tonight and will not be able to give you his best thinking. In your case, for instance, I don't doubt that half of your people are terrified of you."

The industrialist sputtered and his wattles trembled with agitation. "Now see here, Whiting. See here . . ." He angrily punched a button and his secretary popped in. "Miss Johnson," he cried, "take a seat! Mr. Whiting has made a statement. These were not his words, but in effect he says that I'm a bully and a cad and people in this organization are afraid of me. Is this true?"

There was dead silence, and finally, in a small voice, the secretary answered, "I'm afraid it is, sir."

"That will do!" he cried. "Enough of that. Go along, go along with you." It seemed he didn't know the effect he had on his own staff, let alone his audiences.

It would be pleasant to report that the industrialist took the course, had all his employees sign up, and today he is as gentle as a lamb, beloved by all. The harsh fact is that he didn't take the course or have his employees take it. "But he did become more friendly and gave me tea and biscuits. As a matter of fact," recalled Whiting, "I'm still working on him."

While the industrialist is not a testimonial triumph, he illustrates an important point that has been discovered by the Carnegie organization: People who need human relations the most are usually the ones who are most unaware of their need and think their human relations are the best.

Surveys have shown that next to health, people generally are more concerned with human relations than any other aspect of their lives. The purpose of human relations, according to Carnegie, is to help individuals live more harmoniously with themselves and others, to find a fuller and more satisfying life, to break out of themselves and get genuinely interested in other people.

Once a person taking the Dale Carnegie Course has shed his fears and assumed a less negative attitude toward himself and the world, he is usually more receptive toward experimenting in getting along better with other people. As he applies the various rules and sees them at work, he is often not aware that the change is in his own outlook, but thinks it is in other people. The case was stated by a student who said, "The people I deal with are much nicer now than they were before I took this course."

The philosophy of the course is that the practice of the human relations rules should arise out of a person's improved attitude; however, the use of the rules also tends to create the right attitudes, so the rules and the underlying attitudes tend to work hand-in-glove to reinforce and encourage one another.

The human relations rules Carnegie culled from the teachings of great philosophers and religious leaders are what Dr. Stewart McClelland calls "an interpretation of the Ten Commandments." He points out that we do not live in a vacuum, but with people. He recalled a professor of theology who once said, "The kingdom of heaven is a community of friendly workmen." In a Dale Carnegie class, said Dr. McClelland, "we develop a community of friendly workmen where each of us can be our best self without anybody laughing at us."

Usually the so-called miracles that students speak of take place when the human relations rules are applied. The person reporting a triumph generally doesn't get the big sale or win a friend or become president of the Elks merely because he flashes his choppers or talks about the other person's rheumatism or grandchildren; but more likely it is a result of his new attitude; he feels differently inside and is able to *communicate* that feeling. The rules he practices are little more than guideposts. The other person senses the change in him and responds to it. One reason the rules may be so effective is because, due to the change in his own personality, he is able to get out of himself and be genuinely interested in other people and they feel it. Instead of being insincere, it is more likely that for the first time in his life he is being his real self. That is what the Carnegie people mean when they say that they don't change people—they merely reveal them to themselves and to others.

It is a commonplace of the Carnegie course that many people take it for reasons other than human relations, and wind up by saying the human relations training was the most important thing they got out of it. Eugene Fowler, assistant vice-president of the National Bank and Trust Company of Ann Arbor, Michigan, said he took the course to learn self-expression and to overcome "nervous excitement which I could not control." He continued, "But the greatest benefit I received from Dale Carnegie was a lesson in how to better understand people. I must admit now that before taking the course I thought that I already had mastered this problem. Let me say without reservation that often we overestimate ourselves and consequently make the same mistake day after day. With the confidence and rearrangement of my personality I gained from my Dale Carnegie Course, I've had more opportunities presented than I could have anticipated in a lifetime."

As in most other arts or skills, some people have good human relations naturally and others must be taught, although there are few people who don't have room for improvement in this area. The Carnegie files are sprinkled with testimonials from people who were the terror of their associates and employees due to their inability to get along with others, and after taking the training their human relations became one of their strong points. Many others have disclosed that they had to take the course to learn how weak they were in this department.

The emphasis on human relations in the course doesn't come until after the first five sessions, which are devoted primarily to overcoming fear. Then students are made more conscious of other people and their relationships with them. The technique that Carnegie developed and used so effectively is still used: the class is turned into a workshop, the students practicing various rules and making a talk on how they worked out.

For most people the results are internal rather than external, but they are no less dramatic because they often can't be measured. R. L. Weir, Jr. of Bloomfield, New Mexico, said, "Session number six was the one that made me realize and take stock as to what kind of person I really was, and I surely hope that since D.C. I am not the inconsiderate and selfish person I was before D.C.

"Our assignment was to write one of the human relations rules we violated the most on a piece of paper and carry it in our pocket. Though I violated all nine rules, Number One was the one that held me in such a trance. I could see flashing before my eyes like a movie of my life the many times I Criticized, Condemned, and Complained.

"Instantly my thoughts went back to my family. I saw how many times I hurt my children by whacking them on the head for the least minor noise or for just talking; and the times, looking from the corner of my eye, that my children would cower from sheer fright and hate of me because my thoughts were only of myself. That is just to mention a few of the cruel acts I did to my children.

"I can remember the many times my children would ask why Mother was crying, and I had not the guts to tell them that I had Criticized, Condemned, and Complained because she did not prepare what I wanted for dinner, and what she prepared wasn't good enough, or that the shirts she ironed weren't done well enough. . . .

"I am able to say now, with the other things I learned from the course, that I know my family life is much happier; that I really enjoy doing things with and for my children, and most of all they feel that they really have found a father after these many years. As for my wife . . . another life will not give me enough time to make up for all the hurt I have caused her, but I am going to try.

"Though a happier family is one consolation, my job has been much more enjoyable, and my relations with friends have been much more sincere."

To take Carnegie's rules without the course as a background is almost to take them out of context. To be told to smile, if one doesn't feel like smiling, is enough to enrage almost anyone; it was this rule that brought more censure, scorn, and ridicule on Carnegie than any other. Despite his own rule, Carnegie himself took a dim view toward the superimposed smile. In the instructor's handbook he wrote:

One of the most common mistakes made by speakers, graduate assistants and instructors is that of continually urging speakers to smile. . . . In the name of common sense why should we try to turn our people into a lot of silly, grinning Cheshire cats? A smile isn't something you put on mechanically as you put on a hat. A real smile is merely an outer reflection of an inner condition. It is quite possible to be gracious and charming in manner without actually smiling. And certainly nobody, outside an institution for the feeble-minded, smiles constantly!

Anyone who practices Carnegie's rules just to make people like them, or to get a sale, or to influence somebody, has missed the point he was trying to make and does an injustice to the purpose and philosophy of the course.

Dorothy Carnegie emphasized this when she said, "Human relations has nothing to do with liking and being liked by people. If I thought that was the point of what we were doing, I would quit and sell out tomorrow. Human relations is communication between people. It is a modern way to express the golden rule, recognition of individuals, not just a mass of statistics on how one person scored over another by practicing certain tricks designed to give an impression of good will where there was none.

"Human relations is the essence of Christianity; it is recognizing the importance of the individual. You don't have to love a person to get along with him or to live with him. But you must recognize other human beings, as you want them to recognize you, and accord them the same rights you are entitled to as a human being. Treat them with justice and acknowledge their drives, and forgive their mistakes as you expect them to forgive yours.

"As far as liking people and being liked by others goes, that is something most people can't control. But we can control the way we treat people, and everyone is entitled to good treatment. It has nothing to do with calling a person by his first name and back-slapping. You can even fight with a person and still have good human relations with him. Sometimes people need to be challenged and fought.

"Dale said he was sorry he never got around to writing what he had planned as a last chapter in *How to Win Friends and Influence People*. He intended to say that 'there are times when none of the rules will work and you have to throw them out of the window. Somebody has to go to jail, be spanked, divorced, knocked down, sued in court. The basic rule is to respect the right of everybody to good treatment, but sometimes you come across people who won't let you treat them that way. Then it is time for direct action— a trip to the woodshed, perhaps. There are times when courteous treatment is not good human relations; if you are attacked, there may be no answer but self-defense and self-preservation.' "

Mrs. Carnegie said she doesn't care personally for

calling "every Tom, Dick, and Harry by his first name." She explained, "I like to choose friends slowly and carefully, and a certain formality and dignity of address makes it possible to be friendly without committing oneself to intimacy too soon in a social relationship. But first names are used throughout the Dale Carnegie Course for a definite purpose: to break down shyness and establish an atmosphere of easy informality; a workshop spirit, rather than an academic one. People who have not taken our training often do not understand this. They erroneously assume that our first-name technique in the classroom is a back-slapping gambit we recommend for outside situations as well."

She said surveys show that the most important reasons propelling people to enroll in the Carnegie course are lack of self-confidence, inability to talk to groups, and the desire to get along better with people.

"We're concerned with helping people take off the layers of inhibition and repression, in removing all the barriers that lock the personality inside so it can't be free to express itself. We're interested in helping the individual to express himself to one or one million people, his boss or his wife; and to operate on the highest level of his own capabilities.

"We are fundamentally concerned with enabling

people to communicate with each other, not only on a business level of speaking to groups, selling, and presenting ideas clearly and forcefully, but on a personal and individual level also. The pace at which most of us live today, the competition and struggle, the mechanization of life—these seem to result in blunting our sense of individuality. We tend to think of ourselves as mere units in a large group rather than as free-speaking, free-thinking, strong and individual personalities.

"One reason for the tremendous success of our Dale Carnegie Course is our insistence on the importance of the individual. We work entirely on this fundamental principle—that all of us are different from each other, and that difference must be recognized and respected. Everyone has this vital core of individuality; it is up to us to help remove the wraps that swathe it so that it can shine out and be free to operate. When that happens, a person is communicating his thoughts, feelings, and ideas to others in his own highly personal and distinctive style. It is a great release of energy, strength, and resources of personality which may have lain dormant and untapped."

This is evident when students recite what they got out of the human relations sessions. One hears such comments as these: "I see people in a more understanding light." "I learned to control myself." "People become more interesting." "I became a better husband and father." "I learned to accept life and enjoy it." "It saved my marriage." "I'm a happier and more fulfilled person." "I found myself."

A member of a Des Moines class told about a 62-year-old meat salesman who had been working for the same company forty-two years when he took the Dale Carnegie Course. "After getting the ability to deal with people from the course and developing his leadership abilities," he said, "his income started to grow. Each check he received had a bonus in it for his higher production. He was taking first place in nearly every contest the company had.

"After having tried without success for over five years to obtain an order for the Iowa State Fair, he called on the same buyer who had previously turned him down five times and sold him one hundred thousand hot dogs.

"This all took place in the same year that this man took the course. He takes very little credit for it himself, but gives it all to the understanding of human relations and the ability to deal with people that he received at the age of 62 from the Dale Carnegie Course. I am very proud of him. He is my father, Frank N. Cunningham."

Occasionally a student with a wry sense of humor

reports how the human relations rules backfired or had unexpected results. Jim Keane, a New Yorker, reported that he practiced the "smile" rule and the first person he met smiled back and exclaimed, "Jim, you're getting fat."

It is noteworthy how many people originally take the course to learn how to manipulate others for selfish ends—usually to make more money or improve their position in life—and then discover that those things were not what they really wanted after all. They find that the most important thing in life is people, and getting along with them well is the most satisfying reward to be had. Once they make this discovery, they often realize material rewards as well because they have relaxed and become the kind of person they were intended to be before their vision of themselves was distorted by unfortunate life experiences. The operator of an appliance store on Long Island said, "I discovered that the men and women who came into my store are not customers or prospects, they are *people*. When I began to treat them as people it became easy for me to talk to them and my sales began to soar."

There will always be people who cheat, cut corners, and try to adulterate the golden rule by taking advantage of others. Regardless of how much a person may try to manipulate others, most people aren't taken in—unless they want to be; the majority of people are capable of sensing insincerity. The Carnegie course emphasizes that the important point is not what we get out of other people, but how we approach them— whether we're out to take advantage of somebody through guile or deceit, or we approach them in good faith and with consideration for them as fellow human beings.

Frank B. Cullen, a Carnegie instructor with a philosophic turn of mind, summarized the objective of human relations in terms of modern man when he said: "Man will soon travel to the moon—the distance really isn't very far; the greatest distance man has to go still lies within himself. His ability to understand and to be understood is the greatest problem people have in this age."

Another time a Carnegie instructor told his class: "Our lives are largely made up of people. If we live out the teachings in this course, we are taking steps to make our lives come out the way we want them to."

Once the student has been mellowed with the balm of human relations, having first been purged of his fears, he is ready for the next step in his Carnegie training—a stiff jolt of enthusiasm.

PUTTING

5.

SPARKLE
IN
LIFE

Act Enthusiastic
to Be Enthusiastic . . .
the Carnegie Way

ENTHUSIASM is a tremendously important word in Carnegie literature. Many of the organization's officials consider it the real essence of the course. In one key session it is dissected and an effort is made to inject it into the student as part of his personality so he will carry exhilarating effects with him the rest of his life.

Since the meaning of the word is widely misunderstood, it is explained that literally translated from the Greek it stands for "in God," or, colloquially, "God within." In the instructor's handbook, Carnegie wrote:

Do not mistake noise or yelling for enthusiasm. . . . Please, oh, please don't confuse enthusiasm with noise. Webster says that enthusiasm is "ardent zeal, or interest; fervor." Fervor is "intensity of expression." Webster doesn't say a word, in that connection, about noise or yelling or stamping.

To the Carnegie people, enthusiasm means animation, excitement, suppressed fire. One Carnegie student described it as "the fizz and sparkle of life—without it, life's like champagne without bubbles." Once a student's thinking and attitudes have been retooled, he is exposed to the rich juices of enthusiasm. This is the ultimate aim of the course—to send the individual forth with a new-found zest for life, an acute sense of

98

being alive. When a student responds full force, he is said to have "caught fire."

For several sessions a person may deliver his talks in a flat voice, using wooden gestures, going through the motions of imparting information or ideas to his class-mates. But all of a sudden he will "catch fire." His delivery will be as different as night from day; his stance will be more firm, his gestures animated; every-thing about him will suggest that he is in complete con-trol of the situation. He may even achieve that most difficult of all accomplishments—standing quietly after being introduced, arms loosely at his sides, saying nothing, letting a few seconds of dramatic silence lapse before he starts to speak.

The highest compliment a Carnegie instructor can pay a student is to say he "caught fire." Students catch fire at different points along the course, some early, some late, some never; but there is no mistaking this phenomenon when it happens.

Joseph A. Rodriguez, owner of a janitorial service in California, took the course at the Pasadena Athletic Club. His instructors, Virgil Morgan and Fred M. Britto, recalled that Rodriguez was so nervous during the early sessions that he was terrified, "tears would appear in his eyes, he gripped his arms and writhed in agony as he tried to say a few words." It wasn't until

the fourteenth session that he caught fire, at the graduation banquet, when he was telling what he got out of
the course. Suddenly "he was virtually transformed
from a timid, shy, and self-conscious person to a dash-
ing, enthusiastic, and inspiring individual. One could
have heard a pin drop while he spoke. He had the
amazed and rapt attention of everyone in the room, including the waitress. His wife was dumbfounded. She
kept looking at the audience with a stunned expression
on her face and her hand over her open mouth. This
was not the Joe she knew. The applause which he received was deafening and prolonged. Joe sat down with
pride and exultation. He had made it! Everyone was
thrilled by his sensational breakthrough."

Once a person catches fire, life will never again be
the same, for he has caught a new vision of himself; he
no longer is a pawn in his environment, but he sees
himself as a person who can control and direct his des-
tiny and perhaps that of others. He probably couldn't
explain what has happened to him, but he knows that
something important has taken place inside him. He
not only has learned to believe in himself, but his self-
confidence is undergirded by exuberance; he has
emerged from his shell.

It is at this point that students in the course may
start doing all kinds of strange things that seem wholly

out of character—at least the character they previously displayed—and they are likely to startle and unnerve their friends, relatives, and business associates. They quit jobs, ask for raises, assert themselves in business, social, or civic affairs; they go out and make big sales or do something they have been putting off; they buy and sell houses, take a new job, make critical decisions, even get married or divorced. Whatever form the action may take, it often entails a drastic change in their established pattern of living. They have a feeling of power that is formidable indeed, and others can feel it radiating from them. A teen-age boy observed this change in his father and, with wonder, said, "Did you get a raise?" Another chap was asked by his family if he had been promoted. A man who was smitten with unusual force attacked his job, which he previously had hated and shirked, with such fervor that his boss, after studying him quizzically, slid up to him and whispered, "Frank, why don't you go home and sleep it off?"

A danger is that a student may get overstimulated and think he has capacities he doesn't have, forgetting that enthusiasm alone isn't enough and one still needs certain abilities and intelligence to be what he wants to be.

Some students look back on this moment of awakened awareness as a milestone and spend the rest of their lives trying to recapture it. One would have to understand this feeling to comprehend why so many Carnegie graduates go on to devote their time to working as graduate assistants without pay, and often as instructors, with the money of secondary or even of no importance.

The feeling one carries away with him varies with the person, the degree and intensity depending on his intelligence, needs, capabilities, goals, his vision of himself and the world; but it is this feeling that is responsible for the wild and often unbridled enthusiasm so many Carnegie graduates have about the course.

On many occasions Carnegie was able to give vivid and dramatic illustrations of the power of enthusiasm. At one class he taught, a cash register salesman was saying that he had purchased land to build a house and wanted a lawn of bluegrass. "I thought you had to plant bluegrass," said the speaker, "but I found that you could burn hickory wood ashes and where they were spread, bluegrass would come up."

Carnegie, startled by this misinformation, said, "I spent twenty years on a farm, and this is news to me." He contended that it was impossible to grow bluegrass in this manner. The student swore it was not impossible. Carnegie finally said, "I'll bet you $10 it is impossible and we'll write to the U.S. Department of Agriculture." The student accepted. Carnegie wrote his letter beginning: "I'm ashamed to ask this question. . . ." The USDA wrote back, "It is strange, but we had another letter asking the same question. . . ." Before Carnegie showed the class the USDA's reply, confirming his position, he asked how many thought it was possible to grow bluegrass merely by spreading hickory wood ashes on the land. Virtually every hand shot up. Why were they so positive? Carnegie asked. The answer was a chorus: "Because the speaker was so enthusiastic about it."

Carnegie later mused, "If you can make people believe anything as ridiculous as that by using enthusiasm, what couldn't you make them believe if it had some common sense behind it?"

The only time Dale Carnegie ever recommended that his students act contrary to the way they felt was in the practice of enthusiasm. Frank Bettger put the idea succinctly when he said, "Act enthusiastic and you'll be enthusiastic."

G. Alfred West of St. Clair, Michigan, was typical of many students who didn't understand what Carnegie meant by enthusiasm before he took the course. "I first criticized Dale Carnegie's philosophy on enthusiasm as a shallow, rah-rah, back-slapping technique of insincerity," he said. "But now I believe enthusiasm can be real and is the state of being when every part of the body and mind are functioning in unison."

Every Carnegie student is reminded continually of Frank Bettger's advice to "act enthusiastic and you'll be enthusiastic." The author of this dictum could be called the Babe Ruth of insurance. Bettger was a third baseman for the St. Louis Cardinals shortly after the turn of the century, when he injured his arm and had to quit playing ball. For three years after that mishap he worked in Philadelphia, riding a bicycle to collect installments on furniture and clothing.

"One day," as Bettger tells the story, "I said to myself, 'Look here, Bettger, you're never going to get anywhere on a bicycle.' So I tried my hand at insurance and in a short time I was the amazement of the insurance world. Nobody could understand how anybody could make so many calls and sell nothing." Finally he was cut off from his $22 weekly drawing account.

Bettger, who had only a sixth grade education, began answering ads but "nobody wanted me." He tried to get his bill-collecting job back, but "even they turned me down." They still wouldn't take him when he offered to work for less than his former $18 weekly salary.

"In baseball," continued Bettger, "they call it turning yellow. I became so unnerved that I couldn't even ask for a job, and I had a family to support. One day I went to the Central YMCA in Philadelphia and told the desk clerk my troubles. He grinned and said, 'There's a class here that will get you over your trouble quick.'

"He took me back to a room with thirty or forty men. The clerk leaned over and whispered, 'This training will straighten you out.' Then he introduced me to the instructor, Dale Carnegie.

"Mr. Carnegie said to me, 'Well, Mr. Bettger, we're about half through this course, but will open a new class in a couple of weeks.'

" 'No sir,' I protested, 'I want to enroll right now.'

"Carnegie took me by the arm, exclaiming, 'You're the next speaker!' And to the class he said, 'Here's a man who's going places.' "

Bettger says he told the class his story, but they didn't seem to agree with Carnegie's conclusion.

During the enthusiasm section, Bettger said he did a lot of thinking about his past. He had to leave school at 14 and got a job as a steam fitter's helper to aid his widowed mother, who took in washing, in caring for her three children. Bettger said that from his fifth to his ninth year he rarely had anything for his evening meal but corn-meal mush and skimmed milk; as a child he frequently cried himself to sleep from cold and hunger.

Before joining the Cardinals, Bettger was fired from a minor league team. The manager's parting words were, "Whatever you do after you leave here, for heaven's sake wake yourself up, and put some life and enthusiasm into your work."

Propelled by that advice, Bettger generated such enthusiasm that he became the spark plug of the New Haven team in the old Atlantic League; a New Haven newspaperman wrote: "This new player, Bettger, has a barrel of enthusiasm. He inspired our boys. They not only won the game, but looked better than at any time this season." The newspapers began calling him "Pep Bettger—the life of the team." His employers were so impressed that his salary was jumped from $25 a week to $185—a 700 per cent hike.

"I got this stupendous increase in salary," said Bettger, "not because I could throw a ball better—or catch it or hit better; not because I had any more ability as a ball player. I didn't know any more about baseball than I did before."

Two years later Bettger was playing third base for the Cardinals "and had multiplied my income by thirty times. What did it? Enthusiasm alone did it. Nothing but enthusiasm!"

Two years after joining the Cardinals he injured his arm while throwing a ball in a game with the Cubs. It was then that he returned to Philadelphia and subsequently attended the Carnegie course. It was the night that Carnegie taught the enthusiasm session—and Bettger "caught fire."

"Before I went to bed that night, I sat for an hour thinking," he said. "What Dale Carnegie said had stirred me inside. My thoughts went back to my baseball days. For the first time I realized that the very fault which had threatened to wreck my career in baseball now was threatening to wreck my career as a salesman.

"The decision I made that night was the turning point of my life. That decision was to stay in the insurance business and put the same enthusiasm into selling that I had put into playing baseball when I joined the New Haven team."

The following day Bettger returned to his supervisor who had let him go, and asked for another chance. "I have an idea," he said. "Will you give me another chance?"

The supervisor must have recognized the fire in him, for he said, "I'll put you on drawing account for thirty days."

"It won't take me that long," promised Bettger. The

same day Bettger returned with an application for insurance, the commission more than enough to pay his drawing account for thirty days. At the next meeting of his Dale Carnegie class he told about his sale.

The end of that year Bettger finished ninety-second among one thousand salesmen in the company. The following year he was fourteenth. The third year he was first, and he remained the leader in the company until he retired twelve years later, at age 42. During that time he became a legend in the insurance business, a name that makes young insurance salesmen of today palpitate with respect and envy.

Bettger subsequently joined Carnegie on a barnstorming tour around the country. Later Carnegie encouraged Bettger to write his well-known sales book: *How I Raised Myself from Failure to Success in Selling.*

Today, at 74, Bettger is one of the best preserved and most lively men one is likely to find. When interviewed for this book, he said, "I have never lost an opportunity to express my gratitude and appreciation for what the Dale Carnegie Course did for me in business and in my life."

Bettger is the author of a pamphlet used in the Carnegie course; its title: "How One Idea Increased My

Income and Happiness." That one idea, naturally, was "act enthusiastic and you'll be enthusiastic."

The enthusiasm idea is presented about half way through the course—after the student has been prepared for it through the step-by-step sessions that are designed to give him a new vision of his capabilities.

6.

WHAT HAPPENED TO A MILLION STUDENTS

An Inside Look
at the Courses

THE Dale Carnegie Course is given in many different settings throughout the country: in classrooms built especially for the purpose, in churches, schools, factories, public assembly halls, stores, hotels, clubs, and restaurants. Carnegie at one time held all his New York classes in restaurants, but eventually the practice was dropped. A meal added to the price of the course and it became increasingly difficult to find good meals at reasonable prices; the sponsors found themselves devoting as much time to arranging dinner accommodations as running classes. Students often were so nervous that they developed indigestion, not adding to their *savoir-faire* while speaking, and many were so intent on what they were going to say that they had no idea of what they were eating anyway. At the other extreme were gourmets who always complained about the food, and a bad meal, by association, reflected negatively on the course.

Most classes are held in rooms only large enough to adequately hold the not more than forty (maximum of forty-four) persons to a class. To give a feeling of intimacy, the chairs are placed closely together, with just as many chairs as there are students present.

In most Carnegie classrooms the front of the room usually is curtained or plain, devoid of all trappings such as blackboards, flags, ferns, or other objects which might divert attention from the speakers—a bit of staging recommended by Carnegie for all speaking occasions.

At the rear of the room is a table where the graduate assistants (usually two) sit to conduct their functions, including the ringing of a bell when the speakers have used their quota of time. Talks last from one to two minutes, depending on the assignment; there is a rigid rule that no one speaks longer than the allotted time. It is said that during early sessions of the course the bell saves the speaker, and in the later sessions it saves the class.

At the first session students are given books they will use in the course: the Red Book, which outlines the assignments, Carnegie's *How to Win Friends*, *The Quick and Easy Way to Effective Speaking*, and *How to Stop Worrying and Start Living*. Several pamphlets also are distributed. The students are told about the prizes to be awarded each week: pencils for the best speech and the most improvement, and a special-award-for-achievement. At some sessions books by the Carnegies are awarded as prizes: the Lincoln book and *Don't Grow Old, Grow Up!*

The instructor tactfully gets across the idea that there is to be no profanity or vulgarity. If none has occurred in the first talks, he compliments the speakers on their good taste, letting the class know what's expected of them. There is strong emphasis on what is considered good taste; even a casual "hell" or "damn" is frowned upon.

At the initial session students are called to the front of the room, half-a-dozen in a group, and seated on a long table, shoulder to shoulder, facing the audience.

They can swing their legs, put hands in pockets—anything to put themselves at ease. The instructor says something along these lines:

"Tonight you will probably find it easier to talk while sitting down than standing. Besides, we want to treat everyone the same, so please sit on the table while you speak." It is considered essential at the first session that everyone speak while seated; if one person stands, the others might think he is an experienced speaker, increasing their own fear and discouraging them. A California class was put at ease with abrupt unexpectedness when the table with six students seated on it suddenly collapsed. James Mansfield, the instructor, showed the value of positive thinking by pointing out that it broke the tension.

In their first talk the students are asked to tell about themselves, but if they just give their name and address, they are asked questions: Where do you work? What kind of work do you do? How did you hear about this course? What do you hope to get out of it? Did you ever speak in public before? How do you feel about being here? The instructor will try to get everyone to speak while seated on the table, but if they are too terrified, he will let them talk from their seat.

To help students get acquainted quickly, they wear name plates at the early sessions and practice memory techniques to familiarize themselves with each other's names. From the beginning the students are introduced to the Carnegie method of building up "courage" through applause after each speech, and the instructor and graduate assistants perform like athletic cheerleaders to build up a head of steam.

Each of the fourteen sessions is divided into two parts. The first half generally is designed to generate life and heat and to gain experience in addressing the group, and the second half is devoted primarily to the more serious business of drilling.

During the early sessions, which concentrate on overcoming fear, the subject matter of the talks is more general than it is later in the course. For example, one of these talks calls for relating an incident from childhood.

At the third session students are supposed to bring an exhibit to class and explain its use. Most of the exhibits are routine things: golf clubs, baseball bats, tennis rackets, etc. But some students have brought heroic objects. A New Yorker brought skis, lugging them on the subway during rush hour. A Baltimore man, speaking on the importance of having an adequate amount of insurance to protect the loved ones, had his wife and daughter stand outside the door, and at the dramatic moment the little girl catapulted down the aisle into her father's arms. An Illinois student brought to class huge model butterflies to demonstrate the ones in his stomach. Ivan R. Miller of Robinson, Illinois, president of the Dale Carnegie Alumni Association, was demonstrating the strength of an eggshell while he was a student, showing that a man couldn't crush it in his hand; he gave a mighty squeeze, disproving the theory and splattering himself with scrambled egg. Another Illinois man, a farmer, brought three baby piglets to class for the exhibit; the beasts got loose and chaos reigned until they were captured.

Another early session calls for demonstrating an activity. These are usually commonplace things like bowling, changing a flat tire, eating with chopsticks, bathing a baby, or setting-up exercises. An inspired talk on eating peanut butter and having the stuff stick to the roof of the mouth was given by Art McKenzie, who took the course in New York. A Texan brought to class a life-size cutout of a dapple horse made of plywood, which he proceeded to saddle. An Illinois student wore the clothing he had on when struck by lightning, leaving him just this side of indecent exposure. A South African demonstrated how to use an insecticide bomb, but at the critical moment he had the nozzle aimed the wrong way and got a face full of the lethal spray.

Another assignment, to recall "an incident out of your life that taught you a lesson," brings some interesting talks. One speaker told about being stopped by a stranger in New York's Pennsylvania station and asked for fifteen cents for subway fare. "I gave it to him, thinking it was a new pitch to get money," he said, "and then he asked for my name and address. He said, 'I'm not a bum. I lost my wallet and I'd like to return the money.' I forgot all about it, but a few days later I got a letter containing fifteen cents and two tickets to *My Fair Lady*."

Almost from the start, students are encouraged to begin the process of self-examination by speaking on subjects they have "earned the right" to talk about. By the third session they are starting to dredge up things from their past that have weighed heavily on them. One student said his mother died when he was a baby and his father became a chronic drunkard; the boy would come home at night and "I would find my father on the bathroom floor, passed out." He said he was frightened and would try to hide the bottle, but his father would come to and ghastly scenes would follow. "Anyone who has never lived with a drunken person doesn't know what it's like," he concluded.

The instructor handled the situation in the accepted Carnegie manner, thanking the speaker for "sharing that deeply moving experience with us," and without further ado called on the next speaker.

At the fourth session drilling is started for the first time—"if the student is ready for it." An initial step in this direction is to get the students to put sparkle into their talks by use of direct dialogue. Oliver K. Whiting was instructing a class at the Ford plant at Mahwah, New Jersey, and a student gave a talk on how his foreman had expressed disappointment with the job he had done. "How do you know he wasn't satisfied?" asked Whiting. "Well," replied the student, "he made it clear he didn't approve." "Now," fired Whiting, "that is exactly what I have been getting at. You could make it twenty times as lively if you used direct dialogue. Tell us precisely what he said." The student regarded him with wonder. "Do you mean I should use his very words?" he asked. "Yes," said Whiting, "his very words. That's the way to put color into your talk." Whiting later explained, "And it did, but I wasn't prepared for the torrent of language which made the room blue and my face red."

The fifth session, called "Coming Out of Your Shell," is one of the milestones of the course. It is designed to blast class members out of their inhibitions and repressions. An indication of what's to come is suggested by the following instructions in the instructor's handbook:

Ask students to remove their rings, wrist watches, and, if advisable, their eyeglasses.

Announce: If there is anyone present who has a physical condition that would be aggravated by strenuous exertions, please notify the Graduate Assistants so you will not be called.

The class is warmed up with special drills and then the room is prepared for action. A table is set up in front and the speaker is given a tightly rolled newspaper and told to hammer it on the table while talking about something that sends his blood pressure soaring. The class members, at the same time, heckle him, and he is supposed to drown them out with his pounding and shouting.

People who five weeks previously went mute, lost their memories, or couldn't stand in front of the class without their knees banging together, have made enough progress to carry the assignment off, and usually they enjoy themselves hugely.

Dale Carnegie said, "I discovered that this horseplay would do more to help people develop ease and naturalness on their feet than any other method I ever tried. So we have been using it for over forty years. If each member will enter into this session with real spirit, he will get a lot of benefit from it."

Students bring to class a rich harvest of annoyances from contemporary life: surly cops, free-loading relatives, in-laws, television westerns, bosses, unions, etc. More spirited anecdotes come out of the coming-out-of-your-shell session than any other. Many students have had their false teeth pop out and scooped them back in place without losing a lick of their shillelagh. Byron Thompson, a San Francisco instructor, demonstrated how to hit the table with such vigor that his feet shot out from under him and he fell flat.

Annoyances suffered by the speakers occasionally get out of conventional channels. Imagine the discomfiture of an instructor in Ann Arbor when a lady cracked down her shillelagh, crying, "The thing that makes me so mad is when a man leaves the johnseat up. . . ." Following the usual practice of having the student later repeat the same talk without the shillelagh or heckling, the lady at her repeat performance demurely said, "I have changed my topic," and spoke heatedly about a more acceptable grievance.

The excitement occasionally reaches such a high pitch that it boils over and things get out of hand. Charles L. David, a Michigan instructor, advised a student to "act alive and snarl at 'em." The man got so worked up that he "caught fire and threw down his shillelagh, jumped up on the table and harangued the class like a wild-eyed lunatic. The class yelled and cheered his performance, and it was all I could do to stop him and get him down." Another instructor was teaching a Louisville, Kentucky, class when he got himself so juiced up that he hurled his shillelagh against the ceiling and knocked out a couple of squares of plaster board. Martin Meyer had a student in a Hector, Minnesota, class who "got so carried away he started to pound the floor, the windows, the walls, and barely missed some of the students in the front row. We had to grab him to make him stop and bring him back to reality. He told us later that he had lost complete control of himself for those few minutes and it had been the turning point in his struggle to gain self-confidence."

Most students get a charge out of the table-pounding, but some students must be encouraged to let go enough to do the exercise. R. Fred Canaday was instructing a class in the Detroit area when a six-foot-seven-inch logging camp foreman, weighing 280 pounds, claimed he had spent his life learning self-control and couldn't get mad. Mr. Canaday goaded him so successfully that he had to duck a punch that whistled toward his chops.

In at least two cases, drunks have wandered into hotel rooms where fifth sessions were under way. In Lexington, Kentucky, a refugee from a cocktail party nearby staggered into Andrew J. York's class, complaining, "Shay, why don't you people go outside and settle your argument. You all's ruinin' our party; we can't hear what eesh other is sayin'."—probably the first time a bunch of drunks were drowned out by a sober group, York pointed out. In Port Elizabeth, South Africa, an inebriated gentleman wandered into Tony Pocock's class, seated himself in a front chair, "clearly bewildered by the proceedings but determined to see them through. He refused to budge and from time to time would state his point of view by means of an indecipherable grunt. Then, mercifully, he passed into slumber. At the recess, he was revived by a cup of tea given to him by a class member who was an ex-alcoholic, and the worthy gentleman staggered out into the night."

Coming-out-of-your-shell sessions are so vigorous, so noisy, that many Carnegie classes have been kicked out of hotels and other public places. Police once raided a fifth session in Houston, thinking a riot had erupted. One hot night a fifth session was being held in Brisbane, Australia, in the Lord Mayor's reception room on the second floor of the town hall. A crowd gathered in the street outside and on nearby balconies. A man, appearing to be tremendously concerned, was overheard saying, "What's going on in the Lord Mayor's office? a riot?"

When the session ends, the floor usually is littered with old repressions that have been shed, abandoned inhibitions, castoff shells—and real scraps of torn paper. Carnegie instructor James Peabody recalled that after a successful fifth session in Fort Worth, a porter ambled into the classroom, "which looked as if a New York ticker-tape parade had wended through the room. The porter leaned on his broom and with deep melancholy said, 'You all may be learning how to influence people but you sure ain't learned anything about how to win friends.'"

After the memorable fifth, the human relations training gets under way. The next big milestone is the eighth session—when enthusiasm is infused into class members. These sessions frequently are taught by specialists, bouncy fellows who put the students through their paces. Unusual drills make up an important part of the evening's activities. The instructor's manual recognizes the possibilities the evening holds:

Show the first speaker which warm-up you want him to do. . . . We recommend the usual army calisthenics, or jumping an imaginary rope, or double-timing in place, or swinging arms in large circles. Please do not shadowbox, because we have heard of disastrous and embarrassing results. . . . The moment the student's color reddens and his breathing increases, stop him. Do not work him until he is out of breath. If he becomes winded, let him sit down until several others have spoken—then call him back to speak.

Some instructors improvise their own exercises; they may have students pretend to shovel snow, crank a Model T Ford, or saw wood. Jake S. Bailey was instructing a class in Binghamton, New York, and had a girl student use a rolled-up newspaper to kill an imaginary mouse. She swatted with such enthusiasm that the bludgeon caught Bailey in the eye, and he wore the "mouse" in the form of a black eye for several days.

After the exercises, each student gives himself a pep talk aloud, often while pacing with increasing tempo across the front of the room. One solemn fellow startled his New York classmates by exclaiming: "Bernie, if you want to get rich in a hurry, you'd better get enthusiastic in a hurry." Another speaker marred the exuberant spirit of the evening by exclaiming, "I want to be enthusiastic about the place I work. But I can't. I can't!" Questioned about what he was enthusiastic about, he said, "Lying on the couch watching television."

The evening is peppered with slogans about acting enthusiastic and reminders of how well enthusiasm has served others. Frank Bettger's story is told with gusto; it is almost as much of a tradition at the eighth session as was the late Lionel Barrymore reading Dickens' *Christmas Carol* on Christmas Eve. The class is also told how Bettger revved himself up by giving himself pep talks before he approached a sales prospect or gave a talk.

The first half of the eighth session is a talk to inform. Probably no one ever topped a student in a Carnegie prison class in La Grange Reformatory, Kentucky; he used a blackboard to give a talk on "How to crack a safe."

Many Carnegie students remember the tenth session as the most helpful in the course. After starting the evening with impromptu speech training, the "fear and worry" talks are given. Of all the recipes Carnegie concocted for instant success and the improvement of mankind, none has brought more soaring testimonials of appreciation than his formula for conquering worry. The rules for peace of mind are outlined in *How to Stop Worrying and Start Living*.

In a word, Carnegie advised, "Shut the iron doors on the past and the future. Live in day-tight compartments." In other words, don't worry about what is already done and can't be undone, or stew about what may happen in the future. Take each day as it comes and analyze the problem at hand, outline the possible solutions and then take the best one. The essence of this was Carnegie's favorite aphorism: Co-operate with the inevitable.

The fear and worry session probably produces the best talks in the course. Many students are far enough along by then to really let themselves go, unburdening themselves of festering emotional wounds and relieving deep-seated tensions. The instructor is cautioned not to let a funereal tone prevail, but to make light comments whenever possible; even so, there's often enough anguish unlimbered to fuel a soap opera for months.

John Tiffany Elliott, a New York literary agent and Carnegie instructor, said, "I want the most moving talks I can get, because the more the students tear out of themselves, the more they get out of the course." Mr. Elliott, a former actor, sets the pace and mood by telling his class about the time he almost died from a gastric ailment; he works in the Litany for the Dying, and closes: "If you are afraid to die or of death, have no fear," he says. "When the shadow of death is upon you, there is a great weariness and fatigue, and it is very easy and peaceful to say, 'Thy will be done.' "

This is likely to bring thunderous applause from the class, or even a few misty eyes. Then the students rise and spontaneously vent their innermost feelings. One woman began her talk by saying, "Such is the atmosphere in this room tonight that I feel I would like to share with you things which I have never spoken about previously to anyone." She then told feelingly about her shattering loneliness after her mother died: "I felt that half of my own body had gone. I was devastated. Day was as night. I could not eat. I could not sleep. I was most terribly alone. One night as I lay tossing on my bed, I started to pray, 'Dear Lord, please let me have just one night's blessed sleep. . . .'" She later confessed that when she came to the class she had planned to talk about a flat tire that marred an outing the previous week.

In an Elizabeth, New Jersey, class a student asked that the doors be closed and locked. He then admonished his classmates never to repeat "outside this room what I say tonight." These precautions taken, he told about having been a mental patient.

Most talks are less dramatic, perhaps no more profound than somebody telling how they were carrying two cups of coffee and fretting about how they would open the door when, to their relief, they found the door was open, proving Carnegie's thesis about not borrowing trouble.

The fear and worry purge is followed by what is known as "Crashing Through," a blockbuster in the dynamic style of "Coming Out of Your Shell" and the enthusiasm sessions. The type of evening ahead is indicated by a notice in the instructor's handbook:

WARNING

Please do not get us in trouble with the police, the hotel or restaurant manager, or the landlord of the building by allowing this session to get noisy.

The danger spot is when the class does the Joe Louis, Madam Dido, or circus barker drills in unison. If there is any doubt in the mind of the instructor about the amount of noise that will be tolerated, have the drills done in a whisper. It is the responsibility of the instructor to see that the class does not get evicted from the meeting room.

The drills referred to are considered a final chance to blast out any remaining inhibitions, repressions, or self-consciousness. They are outlandish, exaggerated, and usually consist of mimicry. The spirit of the evening is reflected by the Joe Louis drill—the student imitating Harry Balough introducing Joe Louis at Madison Square Garden without a microphone. The exercise concludes, at high decibles, with the speaker bellowing: "I-N-T-R-O-D-U-C-I-N-G in *this corner* at two hundred and one-half pounds wearing poiple trunks—The B-R-O-W-N BOMBER—JOE LOUIS!" A Milwaukee lady got rattled and concluded, ". . . at two hundred and one-half pounds wearing poiple panties. . . ."

The thirteenth and fourteenth sessions consist in part of contests for the impromptu speech championship and the highest award for achievement. At the final session students also tell what they got out of the course. In the course that I attended, there was a wide range of responses. Some said they had gained tremendously from the training, others were more reserved; some said they had gained materially, others spiritually, some said they got both. Everyone said they had benefited in some way. Everyone agreed that it had been an enjoyable experience and they were sorry to see it end.

One member quoted his wife as having said, "Bill, you're a changed person. I don't know what they do at those meetings, but they've made a new man of you." At the other extreme was a class member who said he still had a long way to go to be what he wanted to be, but he felt he was on his way.

One class member who had missed about half the sessions wasn't present at the final night. He was an intelligent person and had appeared to be the most uncomfortable of all when he spoke. At his last appearance it was obvious that he had made considerable improvement in the mechanical aspect of speaking with more assurance, but it was also obvious that he had not changed his basic attitudes. He once told me he thought the course "ingenious but a bit of a fraud." He declined to elaborate. He never really participated in the class nor took what it had to offer; for him the course was a failure because he had failed to keep his part of the bargain by co-operating. The Carnegie people emphasize that they cannot help anyone who refuses to participate wholeheartedly in every phase of the training.

After the presentation of diplomas was completed, the instructor made a touching speech, recalling a scene from Thornton Wilder's *Our Town* when Emily, after dying, begged to be returned to life. Given her choice of when she wanted to live again, she picked her twelfth birthday, recalling how good it was just to be alive, to be aware of life and the little things that make up life.

"Do any human beings ever realize life while they live it?—every, every minute?" Emily asked the stage manager.

"No," he replied, and pausing, added, "the saints and poets, maybe—they do some."

The instructor said that was what he hoped the course had given those who had completed it—a sense of being alive. "My hope is that you will go out of this course and realize your life," he said. "God bless you."

* * *

Many women prefer to take the Dorothy Carnegie Course rather than the Dale Carnegie Course, because, as Mrs. Carnegie says, "lots of women do not want to be in a class with men. It hurts their ego; they don't want men to see them at anything less than their best; they just can't face men in such a situation —although frequently, after taking the Dorothy Carnegie Course, they will enroll in the Dale Carnegie Course."

The Dorothy Carnegie Course—taught only by women—is not "just another charm course for women." Mrs. Carnegie says, "We try to encourage women to enlarge their mental horizons. We look upon the training somewhat as a kind of 'old age insurance.' The chances are there will come a time when a woman will be alone, perhaps a widow. We try to get them to build themselves up in all phases of their lives, so that being alone won't be a curse."

The course helps women acquire self confidence and ease in expressing themselves in business and social situations, but the approach is different from that in the Dale Carnegie Course. A fundamental difference, according to Mrs. Carnegie, arises from the fact that "a woman is interested in fulfilling herself as a human being and will take a course to develop herself as a whole person; but a man generally must have a practical reason for taking a course. He must feel that there will be tangible benefits: a raise, a better job, more recognition, something he can actually touch and evaluate. He must justify it to his pocketbook.

"A woman is more concerned about fulfilling herself emotionally, mentally, and spiritually. She may be a little vague about what is missing in her life, but she recognizes it when she finds it. Women often come to us, saying, 'I feel as if I'm in a rut. I said if Joe got a Christmas bonus and we got a little ahead, I was going to try to do something for myself.'"

While taking the training, many women who have had a marriage proposal hanging fire for a long time have reached a decision, made up their minds about whether the primary interest in their lives was a job or a home, and abandoned a world of castles in the air to start achieving the concrete goals they set for themselves. Others have been able to improve their relations with their families and other people.

At a demonstration meeting for the Dorothy Carnegie Course in New York, Mrs. Marge Weiss, a graduate speaker, told the audience that she had faithfully followed the advice of the first rule card she received in the course: "Don't criticize, condemn, or complain." At the end of a week, she said, "I just had to ask my son if he had noticed any change in me. 'Yes, a big change,' he replied. 'Your conversation is down about 75 per cent.' "

The Dorothy Carnegie Course concerns itself with such things as reading great books and developing good reading habits, and with a woman's relationships with men and other women. Some time is spent on posture and grooming, but the primary concern is with self-examination, helping the students live a more purposeful life.

"If you're going to get the most out of life and yourself," explains Mrs. Carnegie, "you must be a spiritual being along with all the other things you need to believe in yourself and other people. We try to help women have a definite aim about what they want out of life, to sharpen their goals, to pin themselves down. In the end, to stand and say, 'This is what I want out of life, and this is what I am doing to achieve my goal.' "

MEET THE STUDENTS

7.

Who They Are,

Why They Come,

What They Say

ELBERT N. CARVEL, recently elected to his second term as governor of Delaware, has said that after spending over eight years in public life, many of his friends asked him in amazement why it was necessary for him to take a course in public speaking. His reply appeared in a testimonial in *Time:*

135

It is a pleasure to report that training in public speaking is only a part of the Dale Carnegie Course. I am enthusiastic about the way that I have learned to speak more effectively; how I have learned to shed my worries and enjoy life to a fuller extent, and how I have learned to organize my work and my life so I can be more effective in my executive duties. It is my sincere belief that anyone in any walk of life will really benefit from taking the Dale Carnegie Course.

At the opposite extreme of Governor Carvel there was a Chicago youth who gave practically the same speech three or four times. His instructor, Joseph M. Staudacher, finally asked the young man why he was taking the course. "Well," he replied, "I don't talk so good to people, but now I can talk better."

As a third example in extremes, there is Eugene Sample who took the course while attending Howard College. He reported: "I . . . received more genuine enjoyment from the course than any other activity in my whole life. My grades began picking up. I switched to speech as my major in college. . . . I was so enthused with the results of the first course that I took it for a second time. . . . I am still in college. I will finish up nine years of college work this summer. I will have my AA, BS, and MA certificates. With all sincerity I can say that the Dale Carnegie Course has done more for me than any two years of college training."

The wide variety of students attending Carnegie classes was illustrated in the doctoral thesis of Paul Brownstone; he studied ten New York classes prior to 1959 and estimated the average age for men at about 36 years and women 32. "No one class was made up of students in any one generation," he stated. "They ranged in age from 17 to 60-plus; the college student to the retired businessman."

He found that men predominated over women in every class, about four to one. He also pointed out that there was no statistical information on the background of students, but "based on personal observation it can be said this varied from the person with only an elementary school education all the way through to the graduate and professional level, with a predominance of those who had not completed a college education."

In another study, "Dale Carnegie Course Students," by William A. D. Millson of John Carroll University, it was noted that "the median of educational distribution . . . was the level of completion of two years of high school work and that in this distribution were many college graduates from such schools as Cornell,

Harvard, Princeton, Michigan, Alabama, California, and others."

The diversity among students was pointed up in more human terms in a class in a small town in Kansas where a Baptist minister and a local bartender were classmates.

The problem of trying to draw a picture of the average Carnegie student is increased by the diversity not only of individuals but of whole classes. Where there are classes composed only of Wall Street brokers in New York, in Salem, Indiana, there was a class made up of thirty-four farmers and a tabernacle preacher, the farmers wearing overalls to each session. In Socorro, New Mexico, classes have been held for Navajo Indians. Their talks included exhibits such as a cradle board; and the wild animal calls were so realistic, according to instructor Waldemere Bejnar, that "we could practically feel the beat of the large outspread wings of the great horned owl, and the call of the coyote was given several times until everyone in the room gave a little shiver as the goose pimples began to develop along our spines. We could almost hear the soft pad of the coyote's feet running through the meeting room."

Despite the diversity among students they get remarkably involved in one another's lives. In many cases whole classes continue to meet periodically for years after taking the course. Some students in Wisconsin became such fast friends that after completing the speaking course they started a dancing class. Many of the graduates have joined the Dale Carnegie Alumni Association, which is a completely independent organization, not related to or sponsored by Dale Carnegie & Associates.

While the Carnegie organization emphasizes that the course is designed for the average person—although no one knows who that elusive person may be—it is proud of the number of celebrities and well-known business figures who have taken the training. Among them are Major Alexander de Seversky, military strategist; Earl McGrath, former U.S. Commissioner of Education; the late David Goodrich, board chairman of B. F. Goodrich Rubber Company; John Daly, president of Regal Shoe Company; John Fox, executive vice-president of United Fruit Company; A. Lee Whiteside, president of Dun and Bradstreet; Lee Bickmore, president of National Biscuit Company; a governor of Kentucky; Theodore R. McKeldin, two-time governor of Maryland and former mayor of Baltimore. The graduates also include a retired rear admiral, a genuine Philadelphia mainliner, a former Miss America, and other well-known figures.

Many of these people have given enthusiastic testi-monials about what Carnegie training did for them. De Seversky, whose wife took the course along with him, said, "I want to take this opportunity to express my ad-miration for Dale Carnegie's valiant effort to make the American people think on their feet, including my-self." Robert F. Quain, general manager of the Conrad Hilton Hotel in Chicago, credited the course with sparking him out of being a room clerk at the Hotel Roosevelt in New York; he said, "If I were without the confidence that I feel now, I would gladly pay a small fortune to acquire it."

Governor McKeldin, in 1955, sent Carnegie the following letter: "I always have credited my knowl-edge of public speaking, gained through the Dale Carnegie Course, with much of the success and satis-faction I have enjoyed in the accomplishment of public life. I am sure that my ability to present my case to the people played a major role in my election to the Mayor-alty of Baltimore and to the Governorship of Maryland. Now that I have been re-elected Governor, I want to express again my gratitude for the Dale Carnegie Course for all it has done for me, and all it has helped me to do for the people of my City and State."

In the past, Dale Carnegie occasionally agreed to give special coaching to people with special problems.

One lady said she had a little speech to make in connection with a presentation, and "I can't do it unless I can be coached." She was Kate Wollman, who was donating the Wollman skating rink in New York's Central Park. A high official in pre-Castro Cuba came to New York just to prepare for a three-minute speech he had to give; he was later written up by *Time* as Cuba's number one orator.

Before the Carnegie people "upgraded the image" and won the battle for acceptance and respectability, it was common for prominent people to attend classes under assumed names, probably fearing ridicule if their friends learned they were taking the course. Among them were top financiers, successful writers, and a Columbia University professor.

One student used the pseudonym of "Rick Brown." He attended classes with his wife. In 1946 his picture appeared in the paper and Rick Brown turned out to be the well-known financier and industrialist, Charles Ulrick Bay, who had been appointed by then President Harry Truman as ambassador to Norway. Bay, who died in 1956 after serving as ambassador from 1946–53, revealed that he had been so terrified of public speaking that if called upon to speak he would go out of town to avoid the ordeal. Once he was supposed to speak in Bridgeport and found an excuse to flee to Colorado. When he learned of his diplomatic appointment he knew he could no longer duck speech-making. To get experience, he attended his weekly class, went to a Saturday morning speech practice session Carnegie gave in those days, and then joined as a laboratory student a class for the training of new instructors. "Rick Brown" then called Carnegie head-quarters to say, "I'll be glad to pay, but could I attend classes the other days?" His wife suggested that he go to a Quaker meeting and say a few words there—a suggestion he followed. Once he spoke at a demonstration meeting about what he got out of the course and became so enthusiastic that he offered to pay $10 toward the fee of anyone who would sign up that night—a benevolence said to have cost him some $1,500.

Along with the vast differences among Carnegie students, a common trait seems to be enthusiasm for the course. R. D. Morgal, a Cleveland instructor, said, "The inspiration is always present in every class, and each person's improvement, no matter how great or small, is a tremendous thing to him as a single being." Those who react particularly well to the training often seem to develop a missionary-like compulsion to tell everybody else about it. Some virtually become sales-men for the course, trying to "convert" everyone they know. This continuing diet of Carnegie can be trying for people they live and work with. Ivan R. Miller of Robinson, Illinois, international president of the Dale Carnegie Alumni Association, tells about a young husband who was taking the course and could talk about nothing else at home. Seating himself at the dinner table one evening, he noticed a third place setting and chair. He asked his wife whom it was for. She replied, "If we're going to have Dale Carnegie at dinner every evening, he may as well have a chair."

Many stories illustrate the degree of dedication some students have to the course. Don Stitts attended classes in Rochester, Minnesota, and became a graduate assistant; he was so fired up that he talked his wife Barbara into enrolling when she was seven months pregnant. Mrs. Stitts didn't quite have a baby in class to prove her loyalty, but she did give birth the day after her tenth session and was back for the eleventh session the following week.

What the training means to many students is indicated by the hardships they undergo to attend classes and the prodigious distances they often travel. Two-hundred-mile round trips to attend class are not unusual; many students drive or ride trains all night to be back on their job the next day. In 1947, Robert Driver, then over 70, traveled by train each week from Brockville to Toronto, Canada, a distance of 434 miles. Sam Rosenberg came from Australia to the United States just to take the course, before it had spread to that continent. Mario Martins, a South African student, flew over 600 miles each week to classes. An American salesman joined a class in Louisville, reappearing at the fifth session to explain that he had taken session two in Atlanta, three in Chicago, and four in Atlanta—an arrangement provided by the course. Many students have begun their training in such places as Singapore or Australia and finished in London or the United States. The long-distance commuting championship is probably held by a Pan American airlines pilot who alternately attended classes between his Long Island base and London.

For drama it would be difficult to match the experiences of a Jamaica student who drove 130 miles round trip to class each week through mountain roads, often encountering bandits. The student took his instructor, Arthur S. Brueckmann, outside and "showed me several bullet holes in his car and the revolver he carried on class nights. He said the training more than compensated him for his hardship."

Many students have overcome physical disabilities —even blindness—to take the training. An instructor started a new class in Jamestown, New York, and, to his surprise, saw a German shepherd dog in the audience; he may have thought this was carrying the range of students a bit far before he realized that the dog accompanied its blind master. Dr. A. R. Winter, a chiropractor in Fredericksburg, Iowa, blind and suffering from a deformed left hand due to an accident, refused to let his disabilities stop him from taking the course; his wife, who was bedridden, read the assignments to him every week.

Numerous stories are told about stutterers who improved after taking the training. A young man in Pittsfield, Massachusetts, was very self-conscious about his stutter. He showed marked improvement before he was graduated, but more important was his change in attitude toward it. At the final session he said he used to go out with his girl friend and when she ordered dinner he always said, "same," because it was easy to say. Often, however, "same" was not to his taste. After taking the Carnegie course he ordered what he wanted, no longer afraid of what people might think of his impediment. He reported that he also had married the girl.

A stutterer in Fort Worth worked so hard to overcome this difficulty that the whole class struggled right along with him; at the fifth session he got so wrought up that he gave his talk without one bobble, and his classmates gave him a standing ovation. A chronic stutterer in Springfield, New Jersey, made such improvement by the time he reached the enthusiasm session that he told his class that even if he lapsed into periods of stuttering again, "at least I'll remember to stutter with more enthusiasm."

The Carnegie people are careful to point out that they are not professional speech therapists in a clinical sense, but they note that many people who suffer from speech difficulties have been helped by taking the course.

How important the self-confidence instilled in students is in overcoming certain physical disabilities was illustrated by a 33-year-old bank employee in Minnesota. He became ill with a brain ailment in 1955; after thirteen weeks he tried to return to work but found that he had lost confidence in himself and had trouble thinking and remembering. His wife joined a class in Hutchinson, Minnesota, and persuaded him to join her. He regained his self-confidence and the ability to think and remember. He returned to the banking business and today is president of the institution, owning 40 per cent of the stock.

Another who found health benefits through the course was an executive in Mason City, Iowa. He sent his instructor, Leif Schreiner, a worn aspirin box and a note; the latter stated that the box contained tranquilizer pills "which before I took the course were the main part of my diet. Since the morning after the fourth session I have had no further use for them. So I am giving them to you, Leif, because in dealing with men like me, surely you may need them. I feel like a free man, after years of nerves and tension."

The power of mind over matter was dramatized by a factory foreman in Utah. Jerry J. Rose, the instructor, said that at the tenth session the student rolled up his sleeves to show the scars of a healed skin rash, noting that doctors had not been able to clear up the ailment in several years of treatment; one physician finally pointed out that it was due to nerves and advised him to take the Carnegie course to relieve the underlying tension that caused the rash.

What the training means to many enrollees is indicated by the financial sacrifices they make and the ingenious fund raising they often do in order to take it. Barter is still in effect in some parts of the country, foodstuffs or other merchandise being swapped for part or full payment.

A woman in Oil City, Pennsylvania, sold homemade bread, cake, and candy to raise tuition money. A man in Great Falls, Montana, sold his prized gun collection. A male student in Norway made and sold waffles to pay for the course. A charwoman in Louisville took a second cleaning job in order to take the course so she could participate actively in the affairs of her church. Leroy Hill, now a Carnegie instructor, saved dimes to pay for the course. A 17-year-old Memphis youth earned $8 a week working in a supermarket weekends and saved $5 of that sum toward his tuition for the course. A Cleveland student's wife continued to wash clothes on a board instead of buying the washing machine they had saved for, so he could enroll. A short-order cook in Fort Worth saved for four years to take the course.

A touching sacrifice was made by a San Jose mother so her 14-year-old son Richard could take the course. Richard was having trouble in school; his grades were poor; he felt he had no friends, that his teachers hated him. His mother was so desperate to help that she did housework, scrubbing and cleaning, to pay his tuition for the Carnegie course. "The results were tremendously gratifying," according to Richard's instructor, Walter W. Powers, Jr. "He made friends of his teachers and improved his grades. He found that as a result of using the human relations techniques with his classmates, he had all the friends he could want. Here was a 14-year-old boy who could easily have become a delinquent."

Every Carnegie student who attends eleven of the fourteen sessions gets a certificate to the effect that he completed the course. Great value is placed on these diplomas, but at least as much value is attached to the pencils and books that are awarded as prizes for outstanding talks at the class sessions. Except for book awards at the human relations sessions, three pencils are given out at virtually every class meeting, and four others are awarded as special prizes.

There's stiff competition among class members for these prizes, which are considered an incentive to get students to work hard on their talks, give the winner recognition and build morale, and encourage the class members to get involved in one another by weighing each other's efforts. Most prizes are limited one to a student, and most class members usually emerge with some kind of award.

Carnegie students generally place inordinate value on these prizes, especially the pencils, which are kept on desks or displayed prominently. George Sanborn, manager of the Carnegie supply division, is forever getting requests for a replacement of a lost pencil, or a cap with the Dale Carnegie crest. Only recently a former student in South America wrote seeking a replacement of his special-award-for-achievement pencil, noting that he'd had it for years and cherished it.

Replacements are made, but first the claim is validated.

In some instances the pencil has the value of a fraternal symbol. John M. Baty of Marshall, Michigan, said he took the course after being in the same job for two years and receiving no recognition. "I felt like I was 'in a closet,' just another clock number to my boss, the plant controller," he said. At the final session of the course "I won the highest award for achievement for the entire course. Thrilled though I was at receiving this great honor, I could not have been more thrilled than my boss when he found out about it. He, being a Dale Carnegie graduate himself, realized the real significance of this award. He fairly bubbled over with enthusiasm about my potential with the company, and throughout the day several of my fellow employees congratulated me and told me that my boss was telling everyone he saw about my award and the great things he was expecting from me in the future."

Probably the most unusual meaning ever attributed to a Carnegie pencil was expressed by Anthony Hofman, a Czech refugee. Upon winning a pencil he told his classmates: "I wish I could go with this pencil from one city to another behind the Iron Curtain and talk about the real American spirit based on ideals of forefathers—ideals and spirit which built this great country. For me this pencil is a symbol and assurance of a victory of these ideals over dictatorship, and freedom over slavery of any kind."

To help students get what they want out of the course, the instructor has before him a sheet stating why each individual enrolled. For recruiting purposes the Carnegie people have studied these reasons at length and brooded over them. One survey showed that some 50 per cent of the students signed up because they wanted to become better speakers in order to speak more easily in front of their service clubs, in conferences, before political organizations, and in other situations; they were interested in learning something about how to put a talk together, and how to get attention and arouse audience interest in what they had to say. Twenty-five per cent were interested in gaining poise and confidence, overcoming fear, self-consciousness, and timidity, whether talking to just one person or addressing a group. The other 25 per cent were interested in better human relations, getting along with their fellow man, being able to appreciate his point of view and to influence him to their point of view.

These statistics are probably only relatively true. Psychologists know there is often a great difference between why we think we do a thing and our real reason for doing it; frequently we do not even consciously know or understand our own motivation but are taking care of some subconscious, psychological need. Whatever reason people give or have for taking the course, one thing is certain: *they recognize that life has more to offer than they are getting, whether their goal is tangible or intangible.* Fred J. Payne, an instructor in Piedmont, South Carolina, observed that when a person enrolls in the course, "he usually has a specific reason for wanting to better himself. We, as instructors, do not always know his real reasons, but after he has completed the course he has satisfied a desire known only to him. I believe that completing this course makes a person happier with himself. He has proven something to himself that only he can know."

It is an enormously hard job to assess the results of the training because they must be measured against the problems of the individual students. The Carnegie files are so voluminous, so filled with testimonials and success stories, that the overriding difficulty is trying to pick individual cases that actually represent a true cross section of the diverse persons and types who take the course.

Typical of the student who sought and won material gain was Vern La Mere, who owned a photographic studio in Marshfield, Wisconsin. As a result of taking the course, he said he developed enthusiasm for his work; four months after graduating he showed his instructor, George Kirscht, his new Oldsmobile. "It's a gift," said La Mere. "A gift?" asked Kirscht. "Yes," said La Mere. "I made enough money over and above the same period last year that this car is an outright gift from Dale Carnegie." Another man who lived in Vestal, New York, said he increased his income $2,800 in two years. A third student from Dayton, Ohio, found his way into the million-dollar-a-year class of insurance salesmen.

Curiously, those who experienced less tangible benefits often are the most enthusiastic supporters of the course—especially if they experienced some kind of personality awakening. These are the people who say the training performed miracles for them. Typical of their testimonials are: "I have an entirely new insight into life." "I found broader horizons." "I have found increased enjoyment in living." "My perspective is better and more productive." "You find that you are looking at things differently, not only about public speaking but everything. You look at everything more intently, your critical faculties are heightened, you think more incisively." "It gave me a feeling of a new start in life." "I got over a compulsive gambling habit." "I have a new outlook on life." "It opened up to me an entirely new world." "Before taking the course I had been living a hermit's life, wearing dark glasses." "It has helped me to find a new life for myself. I lacked the self-confidence to attempt many dreams and ideals I was seeking."

An instructor noted that "many class members fail to give worthy talks because they feel that they should be relating an earth-shaking experience." This is not necessary, he pointed out. If a talk is honest, that quality is immediately recognized, and it is the talk with the ring of truth that is remembered and shapes lives.

No two students seem to get the same thing out of the course, regardless of the similarity of reasons for which they took it. A Kansas City couple took the training after their children were grown and "the silence in our home was so thick you could cut it with a knife." They said the course brought "a miracle" into their lives, helping them to find one another again. A younger couple in Winona, Minnesota, took the course together and at first the difference between them was remarkable; she was a school teacher, poised and confident, and her husband was a farmer, "frightened to death and showing it," according to their instructor, Robert P. Olson. In the fifth session the husband "really let loose," Olson said, catching up to his wife and enjoying the same level of excellence she had. "As a result, the husband felt the equal of his wife, not only in speaking but in the full partnership of their marriage, whereas before he had felt inferior because she was a teacher and he a farmer with less education."

Edgar L. Bledsoe of Oakland said the course taught him to be less self-centered and he consequently joined several business and community organizations in which he became a leader. "People have begun to speak of my 'natural leadership ability,'" he said. "It seems strange, but no one ever noticed this 'natural ability' of mine before I took the Dale Carnegie Course. I find these things very stimulating and very gratifying, but the change that I feel in my close, personal relationships is the most gratifying of all. At Christmas time I went to a family reunion of my wife's relatives and discovered for the first time that they are a bunch of warm, vibrant, interesting people, and my greatest reward of all came when I overheard one of my wife's nephews telling his sister, 'I want to grow up to be like Uncle Ed.'"

To say exactly what any one person will get out of the course, how long it will last and how it will affect his life and the lives of those he touches, is as difficult as trying to pinpoint the average student and draw his profile. But an astonishing number of Carnegie graduates refer to the course as a turning point in their lives.

A Flint, Michigan, student told his class he had been raised as an orphan and it made him extremely bitter toward life; he wasn't interested in people, and his primary thought was that there must be a way to get even. When his classmates showed that they were interested in him and his problems, he said, he made a complete reversal in his attitudes. When last heard from, he was working with a youth group and reportedly had shed his hostilities and was able to enjoy other people and himself.

The most remarkable thing about the course is not just the variety of people it draws—bartender to minister, laborer to Wall Street broker—but that all of these people take the same course under substantially the same conditions. Regardless of who they are, what they are, or why they take the course, it has a personal meaning for each. Everybody is not molded to a standard pattern, but they are given identical tools to shape their own design to suit their own individual needs. Each person works only from the highly personal set of circumstances that he brings into the classroom, and it is from this, his own life experiences, that he resolves his own problems and fulfills his own needs. This is why Dale Carnegie insisted that the emphasis of the course was to *be yourself,* and he continually repeated the injunction: don't compare yourself with others but only with yourself, with what you were when you started the course against what you are now. The only thing Carnegie required of his students was that they play the game fair, digging deep within themselves for their talks, and that the talks carry the ring of truth.

The impact this can have on the life of the person giving the talk, and others in the class, was illustrated by a government personnel official in Washington, who took the course as a member of a laboratory class for training instructors. The student, a Ph.D., related what the training meant to him in a letter dated April 12, 1961, addressed to Dr. Harry Weber. Upon returning from an extensive trip to Europe in 1956, the student had contracted hepatitis; eventually the ailment was cured organically and he returned to work, but "my energy and zest for the job was not there." He said that "one wise doctor" advised that he force himself into activity. "He suggested that I try something entirely new and challenging. Fortunately, at that time, I had the opportunity to enroll in the Dale Carnegie Course. . . .

"'The first few times I was on my feet for practice speaking, I suffered the same agonies of fright and uncertainty as the novices in the group, regardless of the fact that I had been a teacher in the past, and had been lecturing for years. I had the same compelling urge to drop the project. I stuck it out, however, forcing myself to prepare every assignment with diligence. I recall lying on my old couch practicing and timing my talks, then dragging myself up to meet with the group for going through our exercises.

"Pretty soon, I began to lose myself as an individual with a personal problem. I was living the experiences of each of the thirty or forty persons in the group. I was drawn to them in their little struggles to conquer each situation; I vicariously rejoiced with each in his little successes. Soon I found myself anticipating the meetings with some eagerness. The two awards for excellence which I received by vote of the group were deeply appreciated, because I knew they were really earned.

"Our last session was a sort of graduation exercise; but it was also a quiet benediction. I think that each of us parted, feeling that we had not only learned a lot about 'speaking in public' but that we had experienced something which added to the richness of our lives and indirectly to the lives of others."

The various examples covered in this chapter show that there is no average Dale Carnegie student, as such; but it is easier to pinpoint the average instructor because of a single universal trait that Carnegie insisted each one must have to get and hold his job—a desire to help other people.

8

AND MEET THE

INSTRUCTORS

Sizing Up the Men
Who Carry On

WHEN ASKED WHY he became a Dale Carnegie instructor, Margo Margossian quotes an Arab proverb: "A man's hair cannot be woven into useful cloth; a man's skin cannot be tanned into leather; a man's flesh cannot be eaten. After all, of what use are we unless we help our neighbors?"

Margossian says about himself: "Once a self-cen-

161

tered man, now I am interested in others. Once an impatient person, now I find myself more tolerant. Once in a rut, now new horizons, new vistas, are opened for me. Once suffering from false pride and self-consciousness, now I feel extremely confident and poised. Is it a wonder that I am so demonstrative?"

Margossian points out that as a result of his Carnegie instructor's training he appeared before an official board in Oakland and consequently was appointed chairman of the Housing Advisory and Appeals Board of the Oakland Department of Urban Renewal. This increased his prestige, he says. "What is infinitely more important, I have learned to take an entirely new outlook toward life. Because of this I am much happier and people surrounding me are happier."

Rather than being unique in his effervescent enthusiasm for his role as a Carnegie instructor, Margossian would be considered typical. Throughout the questionnaires filled out by instructors, in connection with this book, runs the theme of service to others.

Ray Bacus of Dallas said that as a result of taking the course and becoming an instructor, "I am a much happier, more successful individual. The philosophy of life I have developed has made me a much more patient, understanding husband and father. . . . The course has led me into a job that gives me a real purpose in life and a fulfillment of the great necessity to make a genuine contribution to mankind."

Mat Casey of Abilene, Texas, took the course originally because he had seen the remarkable results in other people. After becoming an instructor, he said, "I have a selfish belief that I have had a little part in helping over twelve hundred people find a better way of life and enjoy themselves and others more than they had ever dreamed possible. The confidence I have seen develop in Dale Carnegie class members has inspired me to want to help others develop their latent abilities, improve their personalities, and truly get out of life what God intended them to have."

Dale Carnegie & Associates, Inc. have tried to make the course as foolproof as possible through standardization of teaching methods, to compensate for individual variations in instructors. But they recognize that in every educational enterprise the ultimate success or failure of the course depends on the instructor, and tremendous energy is expended in finding and developing the type person they want.

To be a Carnegie instructor, one must be a combination of teacher, psychologist, actor, stage manager, master salesman, raconteur, cheerleader, and counselor. He also is expected to "dress neatly and conservatively, always look well groomed . . . do much reading, studying and thinking . . . have a keen sense of timing and tempo . . . do a superb job of communicating his ideas and feelings to the class . . . never talk about himself but often talk about the class member and how, by taking the training, he may achieve his ambitions . . . give interesting examples and vivid illustrations of the points he is trying to make . . . is filled with enthusiasm and suppressed excitement . . . is never noisy . . . his animation is so infectious that the entire class catches it . . . never lets a speaker sit down with a feeling of failure . . . is a living example of the principles taught in *How to Win Friends and Influence People* . . . remains after class to counsel with class members about their problems . . . is intensely alive . . . gives the class the feeling that teaching them is one of the most exciting and rewarding experiences of his life . . . listens intently to every word of every class member's talk . . . always tries to uncover a person's capacities and helps him capitalize on them." On top of all this he is expected to be modest—he is "humble and gives the impression of modest self-possession. He never appears overconfident but is poised and enthusiastic."

The number one requirement is what Dale Carnegie called a "burning desire" to help the students; he must be intensely interested in each of them and their problems. He "realizes that the greatest service to be rendered any class member is to help him develop courage and self-confidence." He is expected to conduct himself before a class with dignity and, at the same time, to be friendly on a first-name basis, but not intimate; it is hoped that some of his enthusiasm and forcefulness will be caught by the students.

Because of the demands of instructing classes, many Carnegie instructors are so juiced up that they can't sleep for hours after finishing a session—a condition known as "carry-over excitement." If an instructor stays awake most of the night it is recognized as a promising sign that he did a good job, although instructors are indoctrinated with the idea that no one ever does such a perfect teaching job that it couldn't be improved upon; some instructors spend their wakeful hours after teaching in meditating upon the session and how they could have done better. One instructor said that he keeps a file and spends hours after class making notes on each student. Carry-over excitement affects not only instructors but also students and graduate assistants. In the class I attended, the graduate assistants were Jim Wiley and Cliff Johnson. Johnson reported that after the sessions he often read for hours before he idled down enough to sleep; the following day he was still so supercharged that he would stride into his office, firing brisk greetings to secretaries and his colleagues; the latter would shake their heads and say, "Johnson's been to Dale Carnegie again."

Carnegie instructors have repeatedly demonstrated their devotion to duty, resourcefulness, and versatility. They have taught in wheel chairs after mishaps, bounced out of car smashups and hitchhiked to teach classes. When detained en route they have had graduate assistants keep classes in session and then instructed until after midnight, often driving all night long to be back on their job in the morning, buoyed up by carry-over enthusiasm.

This perpetual recharging of the batteries, and the accompanying carry-over excitement into daily life, is undoubtedly a prime reason why so many instructors can report a sharp upturn in their financial, professional, and personal affairs, and their ecstatic enthusiasm for the Carnegie course and their role in it.

To become a Carnegie instructor is extremely difficult and carries considerable prestige among those who know the requirements of the job. Instructors generally are chosen from among university speech teachers, ministers, lawyers, teachers, and a sprinkling of businessmen—the latter often salesmen; almost invariably they must communicate verbally with others as part of their job. Several men prominent in public life have served as Carnegie instructors. Among them are Senator Karl Mundt of South Dakota, who has taught classes in Washington; and Governor Mc-Keldon of Maryland.

In an analysis of twenty-four instructors from the Mason Institute in New York, Dr. Paul Brownstone found that they ranged in age from 40 to 60-plus, the majority falling in the 40–49 category. Of the twenty-four, nineteen had received college degrees: six had bachelor's degrees; five, their master's degrees; and eight, their doctorates. Fifteen of the twenty-four were in full-time speech work, with eleven of the fifteen in a college or university position; and four were concerned with Dale Carnegie activity as their means of livelihood. The other nine came from the areas of business and the professions: two were businessmen, three were in sales work, three in management consulting, and one was a practicing lawyer.

Of all the Carnegie instructors throughout the country, 43 per cent hold college degrees, with 5 per cent of that number having the doctorate. The percentage of instructors with degrees is rising at a rapid rate.

Before one can instruct Carnegie classes he is required to serve as a graduate assistant at least twice, and then successfully complete an instructor-training program. In addition, every year he must attend a rig-

orous refresher course. He is under continual supervision by the local franchise holder and is periodically
checked by representatives from New York headquarters. Dr. L. Gray Burdin, Carnegie vice-president,
noted that "we now require candidates to have a college or university degree or its equivalent, and if the
candidate is not a professional man, he must have
managerial or administrative experience. We also expect candidates to be able to think quickly and ap-
propriately on their feet, with the capacity to draw
upon their background."

The road to instructor's training begins by taking
the course. At the end of every class the graduating
students vote for the four class members they think
would make the best graduate assistants, and the instructor also casts his ballot. Few class members
wouldn't consider it an honor to be accepted for graduate assistant training ("the biggest pencil of all," as
one instructor called it). They help the instructor with
his clerical duties, post awards, act as "stage managers," and send the students occasional "inspirational
notes."

The high esteem in which the job of graduate assistant is held is indicated by the fact that they are
paid nothing, and many serve at personal sacrifice in
time and money. The general counsel for one of the

world's largest insurance firms used to serve as graduate assistant for New York classes, arriving at the door in a chauffeur-driven limousine. The late David Goodrich was a graduate assistant while board chairman of the B. F. Goodrich Company. A Canadian heiress was a graduate assistant there following the death of her husband; she is credited with developing a famed Carnegie drill—"The Duke of York."

Some people become graduate assistants for personal benefit, to help themselves develop further poise and speaking techniques, but the majority seem to take the job primarily for altruistic motives. An instructor recalled that while taking the course he meditated the role of the graduate assistant: "What are they doing? Are they missionaries? After the sixth session I understood—they were helping me do something I never thought I could do. I thought I was hard boiled, but by that time I knew that a graduate assistant was giving something that benefited others and getting it back for himself. By the fourteenth session I had one ambition—to be a graduate assistant."

Those chosen for graduate-assistant training must meet stiff competition to be assigned to a class, and the majority fall by the wayside after one appointment.

Instructor's training is conducted by Dale Carnegie & Associates so it will be uniform for all candidates.

There are no women instructors for the Dale Carnegie Course in Effective Speaking, although women can and do serve as graduate assistants. Dale Carnegie once hired a woman instructor, a university speech teacher, but fired her summarily when he learned that she was teaching his students how to breathe properly while speaking. It is said that women are not used as instructors now because it might interfere with the budding ego of frightened males.

After the initial screening for instructor candidates —which eliminates about 20 per cent—candidates must participate in eighty hours of concentrated instruction, at a cost to them of $300. This hurdle knocks out about 20 per cent more of the applicants. Dr. Burdin said that most fail because of lack of background, inability to analyze and make suitable comments on talks, and failure to prepare properly. When a new instructor goes forth to conduct classes, he has logged a total of about eighteen months' training, covering approximately two hundred and fifty hours.

By the time a man emerges from instructor training he is usually on his way to becoming the ideal Carnegie instructor, vibrant with enthusiasm and good will. He can quote from memory the human relations rules, tossing them off numerically by chapter and verse. He is also ready to cope with the expected and the unexpected.

Carnegie training not only equips a man to teach Carnegie classes but—if he happens to be a teacher by profession—it may produce a side effect by spreading its benefits to the classes he teaches in a university or college.

Sheldon M. Hayden of Santa Monica, California, recalled that he was teaching speech at Santa Ana Junior College in 1933 and "I was not obtaining the results I wished for with the traditional teaching I was taught to use. On the advice of a friend of mine, then in charge of the educational department of the YMCA in Los Angeles, I sent for Dale Carnegie's *Public Speaking and Influencing Men in Business*. I started to model my teaching after Dale's ideas, and I secured marvelous results. This convinced me. . . .

"As a Dale Carnegie instructor I have grown personally as a teacher by using what I consider to be the finest techniques in the world for building self-confidence in students. My early association with Dale Carnegie changed me from the negative to the positive approach. It taught me to teach fundamentals. It enabled me to teach the 'quick and easy way' by encouraging my students and seeing that they all had successful learning experiences. Every teacher in

America would grow and his students would profit if he were exposed to the Dale Carnegie philosophy. As Dale Carnegie used to say to us at the refreshers held for instructors, 'It is not enough to teach people techniques of speaking and human relations. We must widen their horizons so they will get more joy out of life.' "

Despite the personal benefit and satisfaction Carnegie instructors have with the course, they are still paid for their labors. The usual minimum fee for a night is about $30, but this may be higher depending on the locality. Many say the inspiration of instructing is more important to them than the money, but to others the fee is a godsend; this was especially true of hard-pressed college speech teachers during the depression. Dean Ormond Drake recalled that when he came East from Michigan State College in 1936 to join the New York University staff, he got a call from Dale Carnegie his second week on the new job. "I had never met the man," Drake said, "but had read one article about him in a magazine. I had read of his teaching techniques and thought he was crazy. But I was also hard up—busted and in debt to a bank in Michigan. He asked me if I had ever taught adults. I said yes, and he asked if I would teach some classes for him. I said, 'How much money do you pay?' He

said, 'If you are satisfactory, I'll give you $25 a night.'
I had been teaching in Michigan for $5 a night. I'd go
to the Northern peninsula for $10 and expenses. I
almost dropped the receiver. 'Yes sir!' I said. That year
I taught for him almost every night. I paid back all of
my debts in one year."

The instructor assigned to a class is known as the
resident instructor. He is expected to handle at least
eight to ten sessions, the others being taught by specialists in various phases of the course. Among the sessions
usually handled by specialists are number five (coming
out of your shell), number eight (enthusiasm), and
number eleven (crashing through). These have been
referred to as the "muscle sessions," probably because
of their vigorous nature and the exertions required.

Bill Koch, a New York resident instructor who spe-
cializes in the enthusiasm sessions, frequently tells
fearful students that not one class member has ever
died from fright, but three Carnegie instructors have
dropped dead from overexertion—an exaggeration,
but it does seem to comfort some nervous students.
Koch works himself into a high pitch of enthusiasm before classes by reading inspirational messages, walking briskly to class, and doing mild calisthenics just
before going "on stage." A vice-president in a sales

manager's agency, he says, "Being an instructor is the most rewarding work I've ever done. If you've been an instructor, no one can ever take away from you what it gives you." His advice to his students is that "facts are not important, only your attitude toward facts. . . . This course becomes part of your philosophy; in subtle ways and in big ways it changes your approach toward people and life."

Students often are so grateful to instructors that they respond with gifts (discouraged by official edict), notes, letters, progress reports, and Christmas cards that frequently continue for many years. Students sometimes direct their gratitude not to the course but to the instructor personally, in a form of hero worship that can be embarrassing. Most instructors have large files of testimonials from grateful students.

A housewife from Hopkins, Minnesota, wrote to Russ Rosendahl, Minneapolis instructor, after the coming-out-of-your-shell session: "I suppose you could tell me that 'I came out of my shell.' Well, I really did and all of the credit goes to you. You have a great way of handling people and I'm sure hundreds of people have told you. I didn't realize the change until Wednesday. Since then it's been like being let out of a cage, and I mean that. . . . I really don't believe you can imagine how grateful I am."

Martin Meyer, a Minnesota instructor, in 1958 received a letter from R. B. (Pete) Remund, divisional manager of Red Owl Stores, Inc., who wrote that "since I graduated from the Carnegie class in Pipestone, Minnesota, last August, I have been given a transfer and very nice promotion by my company. . . . I know my promotion was due to my taking the course and I'm very thankful for it. This letter might help someone decide to take the Dale Carnegie course. If so, then I will feel I have done that someone a very big favor. I'm sure he will appreciate it as much as I have. Thanks again, Martin, and keep up your good work."

A Michigan student found a unique way to thank his instructor, Charles E. King of Battle Creek. The class member came up to King after the ninth session and said, "You have been so helpful to me that I want to help you. Did you know that you have the bad habit of rubbing your nose periodically?"

A more serious peril than the overly grateful student is the one who is discouraged by his failure to progress as quickly as he expects, or is unable to recognize his progress. Such students are given special attention—extra drilling and encouraging notes and phone calls.

If a student drops the course it is looked upon by New York headquarters as largely the instructor's fault

—an interpretation that is sometimes resented by instructors. At all costs the instructor is supposed to get the student back in class, partly to avoid any bad word-of-mouth advertising and partly because of the Carnegie creed that each person who joins the course must have a helpful, positive experience from it. If a student is considering dropping the course, he may find himself not only besieged by notes and phone calls from the instructor and the graduate assistants, but the entire class may be sicked onto the missing member, petitioning him to return.

A memorable case concerned a New Yorker who joined a class just for an excuse to go to the racetrack without his wife's knowledge. He resisted all appeals to attend class, saying, "Will you get off my back with those notes and phone calls? This is the cheapest $159 I ever spent." A short time later he suffered severe reverses at the track and sheepishly started attending classes.

In a Hollywood class a sugar daddy enrolled his flashy girl friend to polish her up a bit. She attended a couple of sessions and then missed the next one. The instructor called, and she said she had been busy but would appear the following week. She failed to attend then, and again promised to show up the next week. The instructor called the third time, expressing regret at not seeing her in class and saying he hoped she would come to the next session. For the next minute the phone crackled with colorful language—a crisis not covered in the Carnegie instructor's handbook— and the conversation ended with the instructor being told what he could do with his . . . course. Her enrollment card was euphemistically stamped, "Student lost interest."

An average of three or four persons drop out of most classes. Various reasons are given for quitting: failure or inability to meet the payments is the most common excuse, but a few students become discouraged early in the course; some move and can't or don't resume classes; some may have been oversold in that they expect miracles that don't materialize, or they have a personal crisis that terminates their interest in self-improvement. Most students who drop the course give a reason for doing so, although it may not be the real one.

It is estimated that about 25 per cent of the students who enroll for Carnegie training are "course fighters" —people who are openly hostile or have a now-show-me-what-you-can-do attitude. Such students usually can be spotted immediately by their refusal to throw themselves into the training; they must be encouraged to let themselves go and participate—an essential if they are to benefit from the training. Course fighters frequently are the more intelligent class members; they recognize their need for help but seem to fear that being "taken in by anything so corny" would be a blow to their self-esteem, as one instructor put it. Some of them resist most of the way through the course before they relax their guard and give it a chance, and a few never do cease to resist. A real estate owner in a Minnesota class enrolled for curiosity and because some of his friends pushed him into it. He made no secret about being unhappy about sitting in a classroom for more than three hours, and as late as the fifth session made a boisterous talk about his dissatisfaction with the course, adding that he would demand his money back. The following week he experimentally tried the human relations rules, got such excellent results that he was shaken, then tried them again. His instructor said, "He tackled the assignment with such enthusiasm that he came back with an inspirational talk, developed into a vigorous Carnegie supporter, and emerged from the class with a best-speech pencil and two book awards."

As part of their obligation to help their students' egos to flower, Carnegie instructors are expected to know the names of each class member during the first session. When Dr. Waldemere Bejnar taught his first class for the tribe of Navajo Indians at Window Rock, Arizona, he had just completed the name-remembering system at session one when the chief of police, Patrick Nelson, rose and said, "Dr. Bejnar, we know each other around here pretty well, since we are a small community. Now if you want us to believe that the name-remembering system really works, why don't you go around and call us all by name?" Dr. Bejnar, although a new instructor at the time, met the challenge, calling off such names as "Manuel Begay, Hoska Cronemeyer, Genevieve Denetsone, Lawrence Huerta, Ned Hatathly, Dillon Platerno, Edith Yazzie, and Annie Wauneka." He named all forty-four persons present without tripping once. The chief of police stood and said, "Dr. Bejnar, you have convinced us the system works. We will practice it."

Many instructors develop phenomenal memories for names. Ken Connell is regarded as something of a Paul Bunyan for his ability to remember names after a single exposure, and some of his admirers claim he once reeled off 180 at a demonstration meeting, although Connell says the correct figure was closer to 125. An associate is said to have trailed him with a score of 123.

In one name-remembering session of the Dale Carnegie Course, students are taught to remember names by practicing on each other, each one taking a new name for the evening, usually their mother's maiden surname. One instructor was walking in Grand Central Station a few years ago when he recognized a girl student he had instructed some nine years earlier. As she passed him, he said, "Hello, Ruth Kessner." The girl looked at him with surprise, then said, "Oh, you're the instructor from the Carnegie course. Why did you call me by my mother's name?"

In addition to memorizing names, the Carnegie course also includes general memory training. At a memory session in Minnesota, Robert P. Olson set out to show his class what they would later be able to do, by having them give him in rapid-fire order twenty objects which he promised to call back to them. He had another instructor, George Kirscht, up front with him. "We told the class we would 'peg' the twenty objects and then they could ask either of us to call them back. I was asked first: what was object number five? I couldn't for the life of me remember, and neither could George. Between us, we managed to get one out of the twenty objects." Olson admitted he was tempted to try to wiggle his way out of the embarrassing predicament, but then recalled his Carnegie training. "So I looked the class in the eye and told them I had just goofed and that I had been told that any time you laid an egg in front of an audience there was only one thing to do—to step back, look down, and admire it. We all had a good laugh at my expense, and then I taught the best memory session I've ever conducted."

Carnegie instructors are trained to expect the unusual. Several years ago, one of the most senior Carnegie instructors in length of service was teaching a class in the Hotel Taft when a stout woman came in and sat down. He assumed that she was a student making up a session missed from another class, and the graduate assistants assumed that she was someone the instructor knew. After everyone else had spoken, the woman went to the front of the room and gave a talk about psychiatry in a heavy German accent. The instructor thought she was mimicking a pyschiatrist and waited for the punch line, but when the time bell rang she gathered her purse and marched out, followed by the spirited applause and bewildered expressions of the students. It was later discovered that the woman was attending a convention of psychoanalysts and had wandered into the Carnegie classroom by mistake.

Instructors have a variety of attitudes about what the course means to students. Jake S. Bailey believes it "should not be thought of as a tool which we can use, but rather as a key whereby we can unlock ourselves and let the best that's in us out."

Arthur H. Dunham of Des Moines says the course "changes the way people *feel*. Negativism gives way to a more positive, constructive attitude. They feel more confident, therefore less prone to whittle others down to their size, more likely to build others up to the happy level they now enjoy. They learn the fun of giving and the futility, the waste, in taking away. They tend to become more patient, understanding, forgiving, and therefore better liked, and as a result, happier."

Rev. Dr. John A. Witmer of Dallas says that completing the Dale Carnegie Course gives "the vast majority of graduates . . . a real sense of achievement that may be a comparatively new experience to them. This is a real psychological boost. To many others it is like the breaking up of the soil around the shrubbery which stimulates the growth of the plants. It is a personal and mental stimulation which arouses and develops their interests in many other spheres of activity. To many it also means the conquering of a definite psychological inferiority complex and the development of a basic outlook of self-confidence."

What it means to the instructor to see his students "come to life and flower" under his influence and direction is suggested by Jerry J. Rose of Utah. Taking a deep breath, he probably spoke for all instructors when he said: "Instructing is one of the finest experiences that a life full of rich experiences has given to me. The thrill of seeing a person stand up in the first few sessions, full of fear and shaking, and then watch the transformation as the person has one successful experience after another with the tools of kindness, praise, and positive teaching—then to hear these same people stand at session fourteen and testify as to how they feel, and what the Dale Carnegie Course has done for them. It's wonderful!"

CLASSES
AROUND THE
WORLD

9.

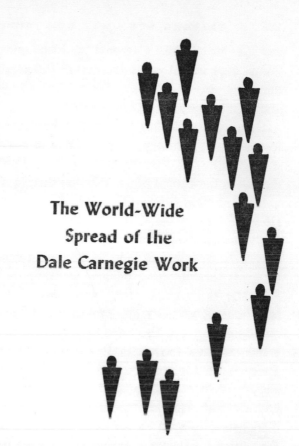

The World-Wide
Spread of the
Dale Carnegie Work

WHEN Harry O. Humm decided he wanted to become a Dale Carnegie sponsor shortly after World War II, he went to Carnegie, with whom he had become acquainted in Tulsa through H. Everett Pope, and expressed his desire. Carnegie nodded and replied, "What area would you like, Harry? Practically everything is open except New York, Chicago, West Virginia, Oklahoma and Kansas City."

Hamm allowed that he would take southern California for his territory, and in the decade and a half since then he has often regretted that he didn't ask for the rest of the United States that was then up for grabs.

At that time Carnegie franchises were to be had almost for the asking. Today there is no "open" territory in the United States or Canada, and franchises, on which royalties are paid to the parent organization on gross receipts, have become increasingly valuable. Presently the United States and Canada are carved into 78 areas with as many sponsors, and there are 177 associate sponsors who have been granted parts of the prime sponsors' territories. In addition, the courses are given in 35 foreign areas in such diverse places as Europe, Africa, Australia, the Caribbean, and South and Central America. Including the numerous area managers employed by sponsors, there are now more than three hundred people busily engaged in forming Carnegie classes on a full-time, year-round basis. Harold Abbott, who has headquarters in Kansas City, has the largest and one of the most valuable franchises, covering some five hundred counties in Missouri, Kansas, Arkansas, Central and Northern Louisiana, part of Illinois, and northern Oklahoma.

Because of the increasing value of the franchises here and in foreign areas, they rarely change hands, but if a sponsor wishes to retire or sell out, his successor must be approved by the headquarters office in New York.

Carnegie courses are given regularly in the 78 geographic areas, and in 1960 classes were also held periodically in over 1,100 other cities and towns. In earlier days courses were given only in larger cities, but the trend now is to go into smaller towns. Recently classes of forty have been recruited in towns of less than one hundred people; in one instance a class was formed in a town of seventy. John Ruskin Hall, retired sponsor in West Virginia, threw down the gauntlet for all time when he declared that a town needed no more than forty eligible adults to make it a prime prospect for a Dale Carnegie class.

Dr. Waldemere Bejnar flew his own airplane many hundreds of miles to instruct classes he conducted in New Mexico. Because the airports often were far from the towns and there was no adequate transportation, he kept old junked cars at the airports to drive to and from towns.

Carnegie sponsors, like instructors and students,

come from a variety of backgrounds. Their ranks include a former lawyer, ministers, several teachers and salesmen (including a Bible salesman), a newspaper man, chiropractor, accountant, presidents of business colleges, and a university president. Many sponsorships are operated jointly by man and wife; several Carnegie sponsors have married their students. Whether or not the wives of sponsors are actively engaged in the operation of the business on a day-by-day basis, practically all are keenly interested in the courses, and the annual international convention staged by Dale Carnegie & Associates for its sponsors and their associates from all over the world is always a family affair. Even the children of sponsors are keenly interested in the work and look forward to these annual conventions as eagerly as do their parents. They form friendships among each other, attend the convention events, and frequently join their parents in Carnegie work when they grow up.

Most sponsors began as instructors while developing their territories, and usually they match or even surpass instructors in enthusiasm for the course. Oliver K. Whiting, a British businessman who had his eye on becoming a member of Parliament when he affiliated with the training, said that for him the course "was a gateway into a Land of Opportunity beyond my wildest dreams. My thought at that time was, 'if ONLY I had taken this course before.' Today, as I look back over all these years, I can honestly claim this was without doubt the most important single step I ever took in my entire life."

The sponsors, generally, joined the Carnegie ranks after taking the course and becoming so enchanted by what it did for them, and what they saw it do for others, that they wanted it to become their life's work. George Kirscht said the course "helped me to deal with people so much more effectively that I began to enjoy people more. I just couldn't see how anyone could live without this training. I became almost a missionary. Finally I became an instructor and shortly thereafter I went into the work full time."

Jane Werner, who teams with her husband, Paul, in operating the Connecticut franchise, said, "We became so interested in the teachings, and in watching the miracles that take place, that Paul sold his own business, gave up the six-week vacations he used to take summer and winter, and now we work regularly fifteen to eighteen hours a day six and one-half days a week, and scrounge a week off after the convention. . . . We make less money but we do feel that we are helping people live richer lives."

John Mason was a writer for King Features in Cleveland. He first visited a Carnegie class to write a satirical feature on the course. He became interested and put off the feature; he went back to the class, realized that he needed the training himself, and signed up as a student. Mason never did get around to writing his feature but became a Carnegie instructor and ultimately took over the franchise for New York City, Long Island, Bermuda and the Bahamas; he also is in charge of national advertising for Dale Carnegie & Associates, Inc.

Dr. Waldemere Bejnar was a college geology professor before becoming a Carnegie associate sponsor. In the former post he found that "though some students responded favorably to my teachings, many seemed to drag their feet and not have an appetite for learning. While attending the Dale Carnegie class I noticed how eager the students were to learn. This idea of working with people who were eager to learn was a very strong motivation for my becoming associated with Dale Carnegie."

Harrison B. Taylor was an instructor of speech at Oklahoma A & M College. In 1940 he walked into the ballroom of a hotel in Duncan, Oklahoma, and watched a young man teaching a class in public speaking in a manner "I had never seen before. At that time I had two degrees in speech and I had taken most of the public speaking courses in two major universities, but I had never seen anyone teach the way this chap was teaching.

"After the class I met the instructor, and I was invited to have a midnight snack with him. Almost immediately I asked him where he had learned to teach the way I saw him teaching. He told me that he had been a student of Dale Carnegie and that he had taught the Dale Carnegie Course in the East. That night he told me of the miracles he had witnessed in Dale Carnegie classes, of the great thrills he had experienced as a teacher, and of the excellent fees paid Dale Carnegie instructors. I went back the next day to my college teaching job a very discontented young man. The next weekend I addressed a letter to Dale Carnegie, asking him how I could become an instructor of the Dale Carnegie Course." Taylor ultimately met Percy Whiting, at that time business manager for Carnegie, and was offered the franchise for Texas.

His adventures in getting started illustrate the rough time many sponsors had in the beginning: "Mr. Whiting advised me that I would need at least $3,000 to cover the expenses of my first Dale Carnegie promotion. I assured him that I could manage that, though

I was completely without funds at the time. I figured that I could borrow $1,000 from each of the three banks where I had frequently secured loans. I went back to Oklahoma to wind up my affairs. Mr. Whiting stayed in Texas to look over the various cities and to select the one where we might have the best chance of getting started with the smallest expenditure of cash. I planned to meet him in Texas in about ten days. I went back to the college and resigned. Then I went to the bank where I had been borrowing. The cashier reached for a note form when he saw me approaching. 'How much do you need today?' was his first question. 'One thousand dollars,' was my casual reply.

"Before pushing the form over to me for my signature, he said, 'You're still teaching out at the college, I presume.' I told him I had resigned that morning. He tore up the note and I did not get the loan. In Tulsa both banks where I had previously borrowed money turned me down for the same reason. I was desperate.

"Mr. Whiting called me every evening from Texas, and when he learned that the third bank had refused to loan me money, he said, 'Well, how much money can you raise?' I reported that I had only $600 in sight; I had found a friend who would let me have that amount, using our few pieces of furniture as security. Mr. Whiting said, 'Bring your $600 and come on down and meet me in Houston.' I caught the next train for Houston. This was September 1, 1940."

Whiting had carefully researched the territory, Taylor said, and based on his findings it was decided to start in Beaumont. "He stayed to show me how to promote classes and also to give me some training to teach the Dale Carnegie Course.

"Mr. Whiting and I spent about a month in Beaumont promoting the first class. We had several thousand promotion letters mailed from New York (on credit). We ran a number of ads in the Beaumont papers, made personal calls on business and industries, and we made a number of speeches. Finally the day of our first demonstration meeting in Beaumont arrived—October 17, 1940. Mrs. Taylor, Mr. Whiting, and I met in our hotel room for a final conference before the demonstration. Mary and I checked our financial situation and discovered that we didn't have enough cash left to pay our hotel bill. We knew we had to have a successful meeting that night; there could be no second chance for us.

"Mr. Whiting knew how important this meeting was to us and he felt responsible for getting us into this situation. What a job he did that night! It was the first Dale Carnegie demonstration I had attended and

I am sure it was one of the best ever conducted anywhere. I believe we had a few more than ninety prospects at that first meeting in the Rose Room of the Hotel Beaumont. Thirty-two people enrolled that night and paid all or part of their tuition. We had enough follow-up calls to make the next day to fill the class. We had collected $1,800 in cash and checks, the most money I had ever seen in one place. We were on our way. During the next few weeks I followed Mr. Whiting's plan and also promoted full classes in Port Arthur and Houston. By the end of November, we had paid our bills, and paid off the $600 loan."

As the course spread to foreign lands, other sponsors had their own problems. The way it is received often depends on the local attitude toward Americans and the United States. In England, for example, it was greeted with some hostility, primarily due to the Englishman's traditional reserve and his celebrated resistance toward any expression of American exuberance. The course also was apparently misinterpreted and misunderstood in its early days, as in this country.

Oliver K. Whiting introduced the course to Britain in 1956, holding the first demonstration at Cowdrey Hall in London on March 27. It was met with caustic comment from sections of the press which deigned to notice it. The *London News* snapped, "This is not for me; I shall go my solitary way friendless and incapable of influencing anyone." The *Spectator,* observing that Whiting had a "faint resemblance both in appearance and zeal to Frank Buchman," said, "This course is supposed to overcome shyness. The student quickly learns a set of ingratiating techniques, 'look a man in the eye . . . write birthdays on your cuff,' and other things more suited to the nursery than the hotel room in which the course is taught."

Subsequently, the *News of the World,* claiming a circulation of seven million, published a series of five half-page articles by Dorothy Carnegie on *How to Win Friends and Influence People,* Whiting recalled, and "gradually the press began to show a warmer tone; by the following summer the *Daily Express* wrote an excellent article, entitled 'How to Talk Your Way into the Top Job,' which we had reprinted by the tens of thousands for future demonstrations.

"The early reaction of some individuals was, if anything, even more discouraging than the press had been; one of the first industrial calls I made was on the chairman of an international soft drink concern whose considerable business in the U.S.A. hardly prepared me for his insular views. 'If this course is patterned on a book entitled *How to Win Friends and Influence People,*' he said, 'I must tell you that the idea is utterly nauseating and I would consider such training a revolting procedure.'

"Perhaps this was not a typical reception, though we found the average Britisher looked with a somewhat jaundiced eye on what he felt was an American effort to help him speak his native tongue more effectively." Whiting concluded, "Today I can count in England over four thousand happy graduates in a land of seemingly reluctant dragons."

David Mitchell, associate sponsor in England, whose territory covers smaller towns and rural areas in Essex and East Anglia, said, "The work is hard and the hours are long. The financial return is less than I had earned before. Even so it is the most worthwhile, the most satisfying job in the world. I wouldn't exchange it for anything." As in the United States, he noted, "people join the course for different reasons. Many are frank and say they hope for a better financial return for their future efforts. But attend a fourteenth session and hear the tributes paid to the human relations aspect of the training. Psychologically it means greater personal happiness to them and to those with whom they come in contact. And there is great satisfaction as well as moral power in the realization that this happiness is not mere chance but something they have helped to create and continue to create."

One of his more memorable students was "a herds-woman of some 30-odd years who had little schooling. She looks after pigs and thoroughly enjoys her work. She is taking the course because she was frightened of the 'educated' people who come from all over the world into her front parlor to discuss problems in pig breeding. She is an expert and an authority on pigs. Having almost completed the Dale Carnegie Course, she now looks forward to these visits and is never at a loss for something to say."

Contrasted to the initial antagonism toward the course in England was the acclaim with which it was greeted in South Africa, primarily because it was American. Dr. Richard Bickel, a chiropractor, intro-duced the course there. He had taken it in Chicago in 1949 "so I could learn to speak in public." He said the class sessions "inspired and enthused me tre-mendously. I wished that someday I could be instru-mental in bringing the Dale Carnegie Course to South Africa. I knew that there was a great need for this course in my country. When I returned to South Africa in March, 1950, I set up a practice as a chiropractor in Johannesburg. Then in July, 1953, by amazing coincidence, I met Oliver K. Whiting in Johannesburg. He told me that he was a Dale Carnegie sponsor-instructor. He was most surprised to discover that I had taken the Dale Carnegie Course in Chicago three years earlier, and suggested that I consider writing to the institute with a view to obtaining the franchise."

Dr. Bickel subsequently took the necessary training in the United States and became the sponsor in South Africa, giving the first demonstration in Johannesburg on August 3, 1954. The following day the Rand *Daily Mail* carried this headline: "Astonishing Scenes at Rand Lecture." The paper gave a colorful description of the event, stating, "The town must have gone mad."

The burst of enthusiasm with which the course was greeted in South Africa was hardly duplicated when classes were started in Puerto Rico by Henry C. Storey —at least, so it seemed in the beginning. Storey, born in Puerto Rico, took the course in the United States in 1953, returning to his native land to operate the franchise there because "I wanted the pleasure and satisfaction of bringing this wonderful training and these fine people together." He advertised his first demonstration, putting his "every last cent" in the venture. Not a soul showed up at the appointed hour of 7:00 P.M. An hour later he was sitting forlornly in the empty room when a man strolled in. "I could have kissed him," Storey said. Then a few others appeared. By eight-thirty some three hundred persons had crowded into the meeting. "I had forgotten that in Puerto Rico seven o'clock means eight or eight-thirty," Storey said. "When you're asked out there and told a time, you say, 'Puerto Rican time or American time?' American time means to be on time, and Puerto Rican time means one to one and a half hours late."

Among the more unusual foreign operations are those in Nassau and Bermuda. An important part of their appeal is that American instructors are flown down from New York City for classes each week. To take the course in Bermuda it is necessary to prove to the government that the course will help both the applicant and the country; the instructor must convert sterling into dollars at the class meeting, with authorization from the currency control agency. The Dale Carnegie Course carries such prestige in Bermuda that the Bank of Bermuda provides its board room for classes.

So, in many parts of the world, men and women from different paths are hopefully coming to Carnegie courses—and experience shows that all of them will receive, to some degree, more purposeful and rewarding ways of living.

10.

HOW THE
WORD
IS SPREAD

Taking a Look at the Promotion
of the Dale Carnegie Course

FRED J. PAYNE, a Carnegie instructor in South Carolina, enrolled Carl Lawson in the course in an unusual manner. Lawson, a repair lineman with the Southern Bell Telephone & Telegraph Company, was perched atop a telephone pole while Payne made his successful sales pitch standing in the street below—just as Dale Carnegie had sold his first and only correspondence course a half century earlier.

"Treeing" the sales prospect so he can't escape, while ingenious, has no place in the official Dale Carnegie sales literature today. Most of the emphasis is on more conventional direct sales methods, plus local newspaper and television advertising by area sponsors. At the same time, Dale Carnegie & Associates reinforces local advertising with a steady barrage of advertising in *Time* and other national news magazines. Usually the national advertising is of an institional nature, to "upgrade the image" of the course with an eye toward making prospects receptive to a subsequent personalized approach on the local level.

The biggest change in the administration of the course today is the pitch it's making for more company business, in addition to the over five hundred firms that now provide the training for their employees. Varying arrangements are made for paying enrollment fees; some firms carry the full cost, others pay part, some reimburse the student on the basis of how well he fares in the course. The Carnegie people prefer to have their industry students pay at least part of their enrollment so they'll have greater incentive to get all they can out of the course and participate fully.

Another shift is the increasing emphasis on the Sales Course, as well as the Dorothy Carnegie Course for women. The former is given only to working salesmen, and claims that its students will increase their sales by at least 10 per cent before they complete the twelve sessions.

In recent years the trend in Carnegie's national advertising has been to feature prominent men— mostly successful businessmen—with a brief testimonial of what they gained from the course. Some of the persons who have appeared in magazine ads include Harold R. Bacon, president of the Housatonic Public Service Company of Derby, Connecticut, who stated that he had thirty-eight of his employees take the course; John C. Standish, president of the Albany Felt Company, Albany, New York, who had seventy-six of his supervisors take the training; Jesse G. Bell of Cleveland, board chairman of Bonne Bell Cosmetics, who had nearly one hundred of his employees and all the company's executives take the course. Others featured in recent testimonial ads include L. C.

Jacobson, vice-president of Del E. Webb Construction Company, one of the nation's largest construction firms; Henry Blackstone, president of the Servo Corporation of America; Thomas C. Burrows, general sales manager of Anheuser-Busch, Inc.; Governor Paul Fannin of Arizona; Governor Elbert N. Carvel of Delaware; Harry B. Warner, president of B. F. Goodrich Chemical Company; Mrs. Josephine Bay Paul, president of A. M. Kidder Company; Mrs. Mary G. Roebling, chairman of the board and president of the Trenton Trust Company; Charles W. Staab, executive vice-president and business manager of *The Cincinnati Enquirer;* M. G. O'Neil, president of General Tire & Rubber Company; Robert S. Bell, president of Packard Bell Electronics Company; and Kemmons Wilson, chairman of the board of Holiday Inns of America, Inc.

In addition, ads may challenge the reader with such searing questions as: "What does your boss think when your name comes up for promotion?" "Are you too good to lose and not good enough to promote?" "What does the boss *think* when you say, 'I need a raise'?" Copy for the last ad continues: "Somewhere every day a man works up his courage to ask for a raise—then blunders through the ordeal. Seldom does he know how to talk to his employer in terms of mutual interests."

Here's another ad calculated to make a man stop and think: "Is anybody listening? . . . when you speak your views . . . when you try to move others . . . when you have a better idea?" And what red-blooded male wouldn't blanch (and be goaded to action) when faced with this stopper: "Do you belong to the silent majority?"

If the reader appraises himself in the light of these jolting questions, he is not left to stew in his own juice but is given the answer to how he can help himself. Jesse G. Bell, for example, says, "The hours I devoted to completing the Dale Carnegie Course were the most helpful and valuable of my life. In addition to the important ability to speak on your feet, you develop a spirit and attitude that benefits all your relationships." There is also a message of hope from Alfred J. Roach, sales manager of Edwards and Hanly, a Hempstead, New York, brokerage firm. He says: "I had my doubts about the Dale Carnegie Course when I enrolled in January, 1957. . . . During the twelve weeks of the course my production increased over 100 per cent. And that's not all! Two months later I was promoted to sales manager of the mutual funds department."

The Carnegie ads have proved to be extremely effective. The highly respected Starch Reports, research authority of the advertising field, have found that the ads have an exceptionally high readership and public acceptance.

This type of advertising, by emphasizing the stature of some of the Carnegie graduates, undoubtedly has elevated the "image" of the course and made selling easier, but the majority of enrollees still come from referrals—as a result of the recommendation of a friend or relative. Many people, however, sign up merely because they notice the change in another person and want the same thing for themselves. The enthusiasm of Carnegie students and graduates for the course accounts for many referrals, and throughout the training, students are urged to submit names of relatives, friends, business acquaintances, and others whom they think the course would help. These prospects then are subjected to a lively broadside of promotional literature urging them to join a class.

John Cooper, vice-president in charge of field operations and administration for Dale Carnegie & Associates, estimates that up to 81 per cent of all enrollees join the classes as a result of referrals. Mrs. Patricia G. Evans, Chicago sponsor, kept records for many years and found that 70.4 per cent of her students "were a direct result of referrals from employers, associates, friends, and members of families who were enrollees and graduates."

One woman, who borrowed small sums of money from friends to enroll, talked at least fifteen or twenty people into signing up. An assistant buyer for a Kansas City department store said she had just been transferred from Wichita, and her buyer there recommended that she take the Dale Carnegie Course when she got to Kansas City, "even if you have to mortgage your home to do it." A Utah woman was enrolled by her husband; later she said it had helped her overcome a severe inferiority complex and enabled her to enjoy being with people.

Billy Cope, a car salesman who took the course in Wichita Falls, wrote to R. G. Sanderson, the sponsor in Dallas, stating that it had meant a $400 a month increase in earnings to him and placed him at the top of his sales category. "To give you some idea of the respect our organization has for this training," he added, "our dealer, Melvin Roberts, and his wife are graduates, along with our office manager and service manager. Six of our salesmen are enrolling in your next class because of what they have seen it do for me."

It is not uncommon for people to take the course

and then enroll their entire families. Charles Nishioka
of Honolulu finished the training and sent his wife,
son, daughter, younger brother, and four of his employees; he refers to the course as a turning point in his
life, crediting it with increasing business at his service
station by 30 per cent. An entire Wisconsin family
enrolled in the same class—father, mother, son,
daughter-in-law, and two daughters, one of the latter
only 10 years old. David Hodel of Roanoak, Illinois,
and his wife took the course, along with their son, two
daughters, and their children's spouses. Many husbands and wives enroll together, taking advantage of
special family rates, and often a wife will sign up as a
result of her husband's enthusiastic reports and the
visible changes in him. Mette and Carl Jacobs took
the course in New York after he signed up and gave
it to her as a Christmas present.

A classic case of a referral by example concerned
a lame instructor, Merrill Ross, of Connecticut who
fell and shattered a leg and was in a full-length body
cast for six months during 1960. Paul and Jane
Werner, the sponsors, said Ross "never once complained, but lived each moment at a time. He was such
an example that the man who shared the hospital
room with him came to the course and enrolled as

soon as he was released from the hospital, and so did his wife."

Most people who take the course in large cities, regardless of where they heard about it or what stimulated their interest, actually sign up at demonstration meetings. These are built around a strong sales pitch and student speakers who have taken the course telling what it did for them. This technique was developed by Dale Carnegie, who without extensive use of the direct selling methods often used today signed up remarkable numbers of students. Approximately 60 to 70 per cent of the persons who attend "demos," as they're called, eventually enroll.

Demonstration meetings are the primary recruiting device in larger cities like New York, Chicago, Detroit, and Los Angeles; they are announced through local newspaper ads that proclaim what the training will do for YOU! In smaller communities, and through much of the Middle West, the course is sold almost exclusively through service clubs: Kiwanis, Lions, Rotary, etc. Many Carnegie sponsors work with and through these service organizations to promote Dale Carnegie classes as a community project; this has become a tremendously important part of the business.

In recent years direct selling also has become increasingly important as a sales tool. The course is

now sold by many men who represent the sponsors
and go out and make direct calls; these salesmen don't
rap on doors at random but generally follow up leads
supplied to them. The Boston operation is based almost exclusively on direct selling. Philadelphia uses
both direct selling and demonstrations. Other communities use various combinations of techniques that
have proved effective in their particular areas.

The difference in the appeal of the sales pitch to
the type of audience to which it is directed was illustrated when one of the top demonstration men from
another part of the country once tried to sell a New
York audience, and out of about one hundred people
present only five enrolled.

On another occasion, an instructor was conducting
a demonstration in the Laurentian Hotel in Ottawa,
Canada. A crowd of two hundred and fifty showed
up and the session was going well, with good graduate
speakers and a responsive audience. A highlight of
the evening was the awarding of a Dale Carnegie book
as a door prize. The winner was a pregnant lady; she
was asked to say a few words but declined. With
mild persuasion she changed her mind. Upon standing
up she blurted out, "I have a feeling my baby is going
to be born this minute." She was hustled out promptly,
with no attempt to enroll her.

After the session the instructor asked how many had signed up. The answer staggered him: "Nobody."

"I felt like dying," he said. "I was so shaken that I went straight to bed, pulling the covers over my head." The next day he got a phone call from the graduate assistant, who exclaimed, "It was the best demo ever." The instructor then asked why, saying, "Nobody signed up." "Yes they did," came the reply. "It was a wonderful response. But you know that here people won't be pressured into doing things and they have to think them over first. We've been getting calls from people signing up all morning."

While demonstration meetings have emerged as a conventional and standardized sales technique for the course, they began as something between a revival meeting and a riot following the fabulous success of *How to Win Friends and Influence People.*

II.

HIS
ASTONISHING
BOOK

The Story of *How to Win Friends* and *Influence People*

DALE HILL, sponsor of the Carnegie course in San Francisco, was conducting a demonstration meeting in the Sir Francis Drake Hotel in the spring of 1953 when an extremely attractive woman in her late thirties interrupted. In broken English she apologized for the interruption but said she had to catch a train. "When I see that great name Dale Carnegie in the newspaper, I had to come," she said.

She explained that she had been in a prisoner-of-war camp for eighteen months during World War II, was beaten and lived in squalor. There were twenty-six others. Somebody had a copy of *How to Win Friends*

213

and Influence People. They never stopped reading it. It
was passed from one to the other. Each person read it
dozens of times until it fell apart. She said the book
gave them hope, saved their sanity. Tears streaming
down her face, she left the meeting.

This story illustrates the impact that *How to Win
Friends* had on countless lives. Since its publication
in 1936 it has spread its message over the globe. The
title has become part of the language: it comes out
in speeches at the United Nations; it is in newsletters,
the public press; it is mouthed by orators. How many
friends it has won for how many people and who
has been influenced by whom is a matter of conjecture,
but the book has won for Dale Carnegie international
fame that may outlast his stone memorial at Belton,
Missouri, and in some quarters of the globe his fame
is illuminated by idolatry. Only recently an administrative assistant at Dale Carnegie & Associates in
New York received a letter from a youth in India
thanking her for having sent him a picture of Dale
Carnegie. Signing himself only as "Graenauathau,"
he wrote: "I did not know that Mr. Dale Carnegie is
dead. Such great men can never die. Whenever I read
his books—I am reading a chapter in each of his
books, *How to Win Friends and Influence People* and
How to Stop Worrying and Start Living, every day—

I imagine that Mr. Carnegie is speaking to me. Mr. Carnegie will live for ever—as long as English language lives. Both of the books referred to above will be my prayer books as long as I live. I have framed the photo and kept it on my table. I am sure that Mr. Carnegie will guide me and inspire me throughout my life in this weary world."

When Premier U Nu of Burma announced that he intended to visit the United States a few years ago, he said that as a result of having read *How to Win Friends,* Dale Carnegie was the man he most wanted to meet while in the United States. Unfortunately he never got to meet Carnegie. During his Washington visit, Premier Nu addressed the National Press Club, saying he had translated for publication in Burma Dale Carnegie's *How to Win Friends,* as well as Karl Marx's *Das Kapital.* Asked which of the two works was the most popular in Burma, the *New York Times* reported, Premier Nu replied that "of course Dale Carnegie outsold Karl Marx."

Carnegie's fame that followed in the wake of the world-wide dispersal of *How to Win Friends* has often been a blessing for those who carry on under the Carnegie banner. Dr. Harry Weber, a Carnegie instructor previously mentioned in these pages, recalled that when *How to Win Friends* came out he "was greatly fascinated by the book; read, reread, and then spot-read it all within one month." At that time he visited the home of a girl friend and the book came up during the dinner conversation. His hostess, the wife of an important school official in Pennsylvania, was complimented by Weber, and she chided him, "Don't use any of those tricks on me. I have read the book too, don't forget."

Dr. Weber said that after having read the book he wanted to take the Carnegie course, but a decade passed with no opportunity to do so. Having been a debate coach, he wanted to become a Carnegie teacher but learned that he would first have to take the course. He and a friend resolved to take it at first opportunity, and they went to a demonstration meeting in the Statler Hotel in Washington, D.C., with that in mind. Both of them found the session inspiring, and his friend enrolled. "I do not know what suddenly came over me," Dr. Weber said. "I refused to sign up. It is difficult to explain . . . years and years I had looked forward to getting into a class and maybe someday becoming an instructor, and here I was on the threshold and refusing to enter. Some excuses I used at the time were: 'I do not have the money; I might be changing jobs out of Washington; I don't believe the Dale Carnegie Course would do me any good; the Dale Carnegie Course is not what I thought it was.' "

Finally, due to the enthusiasm of his friend, he did enroll. "Even then I made one stipulation and I have no idea even to this day why I made it: 'None of my friends or my office are to learn of my taking the course.' Perhaps I was ashamed to be a student; perhaps I thought the course was good stuff but that the public still looked down on it; I have no justification for it. Maybe I thought my friends would think I had belittled myself. This secrecy was maintained but it did not mar my liking the course. Probably it was also proof that I needed the course. I am not able to draw a firm conclusion, but I believe my subconscious mind was still carrying that chiding remark which my hostess at the dinner had made back in 1936: 'Don't use any of those tricks on me.' While I had refused to admit the *How to Win* book was a bunch of tricks, probably I was harboring the thought. Fortunately at one of the final sessions of the Dale Carnegie Course, one of our instructors, Mr. Oliver K. Whiting, said in the course of his commenting, 'The Dale Carnegie Course is not a bag of tricks but a Way of Life.' This touched something in me and gave me a higher sense of values regarding the whole procedure. Gradually I began telling my friends and urging them to get in on the profit to themselves. Now I wish that no human being would have to live his life without the benefit of the Dale Carnegie Course."

How to Win Friends wasn't consciously planned as much as it just evolved. The book had its inception in Carnegie's courses which began in 1912. He recalled the origin of the book during a demonstration talk in New York the year it came out, 1936, explaining that students would come to him only if "you can give them precisely what they want—when you give them something they can use tomorrow to increase their income, to increase their effectiveness in their business and social contacts.

"So I had to be practical. I went over to the public library and to my astonishment I couldn't find a single book written on the subject. But I read a lot of magazine articles. Finally I hired a trained research man. He spent eight hours a day for eighteen solid months plowing through countless hundreds of tomes of psychology, reading countless thousands of magazine articles—reading everything that had the remotest bearing on the subject of how to win friends and influence people.

"Finally, I said to him: 'I'll tell you what I want you to do. I want you to read the biographies of the

great men of all ages. I am determined to spare no
time, expense, or money to discover how the great
men of all ages were able to make friends and influence
people. I remember he read twenty biographies of
Theodore Roosevelt alone. He read the biographies
of everybody from Thomas Edison to Cleopatra. . . .

"Well, I'd come to the classes and I'd say to the
business men and women: 'Here's what Theodore
Roosevelt did; and this is what Benjamin Franklin
did; this is what Lincoln said—Socrates, Plato.

" 'Let's go out and try this in your everyday business
and social contacts. Try it on your customers, employers, on your family, and come back a week from
tonight and talk about what the results were!' Well,
you ought to have seen the enthusiasm. They came to
class with something they wanted to talk about because they had had experiences that were stewing
within them. And they got up and forgot all about
the fact that they were making a speech, and so did
the other students

"Then, of course, we began to discuss it. . . . So
you see I have been working in a human laboratory—
a laboratory of human relations almost every night
in the year for twenty-five years. And the funny part
of it is that, so far as I know, it is the only laboratory
in human relations that the world has even known.

I didn't organize it because of my brilliance. We just organized it because it seemed to be the natural thing to do. We never even thought about what we were doing."

In the beginnning, Carnegie was concerned only with helping his students to speak more effectively in public. But in practice he found the need for a greater personal relationship between the students and the people with whom they came in contact. Out of this developed the human relations aspect of the course, and eventually the emphasis of the training was shifted to encompass human relations, using public speaking as the means to that end. The goal was to teach the students to adapt themselves better to a variety of social situations. This, in turn, inspired Carnegie to develop his monumental best seller, *How to Win Friends and Influence People*. Later his *How to Stop Worrying and Start Living* gave greater emphasis to the personal nature of the course, continuing to use public speaking as the teaching tool.

Dale Carnegie originally planned *How to Win Friends and Influence People* as a textbook for his students and intended to publish the book himself for this purpose only, not for the general public. However, Leon Shimkin, now chairman of the board of Simon & Schuster, was at that time a junior partner and general manager of that prominent New York publishing firm, and a student in a Dale Carnegie Course given for executives in Larchmont, New York. He persuaded Carnegie to allow Simon & Schuster to publish the book. Carnegie agreed, on condition that he might buy the books at cost for his students.

Historically, *How to Win Friends* touched off a revolution in the publishing business, revealing the tremendous market in America for self-help books. Part of its popularity was probably due to the title, which also was unusual in its day. This was an era of catchy book titles, like *Live Alone and Like It, Wake Up and Live,* and *Orchids on Your Budget.*

"How to Make Friends and Influence People" was the title originally supplied by Carnegie, but it was considered only a working title. Everyone concerned thought it inappropriate and too long. Editors and their assistants spent weeks trying to find a better one, but nothing seemed to fit the book as well as Carnegie's suggested title. In the end it was adopted, with "Win" being substituted for "Make" because the artist designing the dust cover wanted a shorter word.

At the time the book came out, it was considered primarily for the humble man. It wasn't realized then that people of all ages in all classes and occupations had trouble adjusting to life and getting along with other people. Shortly after the book was released, a two-year survey by the University of Chicago, the American Association for Adult Education, and the United YMCA Schools revealed facts that dovetailed with Carnegie's beliefs: people were found to be interested first in their health, and second in social skills —getting along with and influencing other people.

Carnegie never expected the book to have a big sale. He looked upon it primarily as a textbook for his classes, once commenting, "I'll be surprised if it sells five thousand copies."

He took it so casually that he had originally intended to add a chapter on taking direct action (a punch in the nose, a trip to the woodshed, etc.) if the rules outlined didn't work, but his editorial advisers felt this would largely negate the rest of the book. Carnegie was planning one of his long vacations in the Canadian Rockies; he decided that when it was time for him to leave, he would put a period wherever he was in the manuscript and that would be the end. And that was how the final chapter on taking direct action never came to be written.

The book was released in October, 1936, with a printing of five thousand copies selling for $1.98. In the beginning it was virtually ignored by both critics and public, although hard-hitting mail-order ads by

Simon & Schuster brought an excellent and immediate response—the only clue to the book's potentiality. About December it started to roll and soon was selling at a 5,000-a-day clip, continuing at that pace for some two years. Shimkin obtained a list of everyone who had taken the course and sent them letters announcing the book's publication. This brought an extraordinary response in sales, many of them personal orders, often followed by quantity orders for copies for friends and relatives. Companies frequently bought hundreds of copies, distributing them to their employees, especially salesmen. Between a ground swell of word-of-mouth publicity and newspaper ads, the book soared to new sales records; within a year more than a half million copies had been sold—a record for a nonfiction book at that time.

From the moment the book caught on, adverse criticism and snide remarks, favorable reviews and veneration, alike seemed to have no effect but to increase sales. Sinclair Lewis, the blood-letting author of *Main Street* and *Babbitt,* enraged by such enobling advice as "smile," snarled that the Carnegie principles ought to enable any student to make more money "though there is the slight trouble that they may make it difficult for the student himself, and impossible for his wife to live with him." The late James Thurber wrote that the "disingenuities" in Carnegie's set of rules and case histories stood out "like ghosts at a banquet." The *New York Times* blandly commented, "By all means let us follow the sensible advice so cheerfully offered. . . . Improvement in tact and imagination may indeed make us more efficient and agreeable."

Carnegie was vacationing in Europe when the book started to run wild in sales, and in a series of frenzied letters and wires he was advised of what was happening. Ecstatic, he returned home. Overnight he was world famous. Within six months he had made $125,000 and was in demand for lectures, radio shows, and magazine articles. His first check from Simon & Schuster was for $90,000 and his secretary, Mrs. Abigail Connell, recalled that he kept it on his desk for about three days, looking at it, not seeming to know what to do with it.

Shimkin credits the timing of the book with much of its success. It came out toward the end of the depression, he notes. "People were looking forward to better days, and having gone through a long period of depression, they were searching for a positive philosophy."

As sales roared on, cracking records, letters came from readers by the tens of thousands. They were sad, humorous, pathetic, hilarious, tragic, sardonic, whimsical, hopeful, maudlin, inspiring, vicious, grateful. The majority sang the same theme: "You have changed my life. . . ." Carnegie read most of the letters, answering those that particularly impressed him; he was especially interested in letters from children—if they had a spark in them—and often wrote many pages in a single reply.

As a result of the fame that followed the massive sales of *How to Win Friends,* the Dale Carnegie Course spread from the New York area all over the United States and ultimately throughout the world. H. Everett Pope started the course on the highroad to national sales. The operator of a business school in Tulsa, Pope was having trouble due to the depression. "In the spring of 1939 we had eighteen girl graduates from my school for whom we couldn't find jobs. Right at that time I had just finished reading *How to Win Friends and Influence People,* and I thought it contained the answer to our problem. Each day I would assemble the girls and read the book to them, chapter by chapter. Then when a call came in, we would discuss the rules on how best to apply for the job. Soon the girls were all placed in positions, and I wrote to Mr. Carnegie and told him what we had been doing. He replied, 'You haven't any right to teach the Dale

Carnegie Course.' I went to New York City and persuaded him to let us train an instructor. We sent an attorney, and he was personally trained by Mr. Carnegie. We became the first business school sponsor in the fall of 1939."

The book was responsible for many students taking the course. Typical was Edward Dwyer, proprietor of Dwyer's Elbow Room in Newark, New Jersey—probably the only saloon with three separate bars under one roof. Dwyer was taking a train from Ohio to his home a few years after the book appeared and at a newsstand he hastily grabbed several publications, including a twenty-five-cent copy of *How to Win Friends*. He became so interested that he enrolled in a class in New Jersey. It made such an impression on him that in the fall term he enrolled his one-armed colored porter Junius, the short-order cook, and the bartender; and the following spring term he enrolled the other bartenders and the bouncers. He also required all his bartenders and waiters to carry a paperback copy of *How to Win Friends* in their hip pocket. Dwyer said business went up at least 10 per cent, which he attributed to Carnegie's book.

The enthusiasm generated by *How to Win Friends* reached its highest peak in New York. At the same time the book was being advertised in full-page ads, Carnegie ran full-page ads for demonstration meetings of his course. Some of these sessions attracted as many as six thousand people. An epic demonstration, at the Hotel Astor, drew about twenty-five hundred persons who wanted to win friends and influence people. Percy Whiting said he doesn't remember anything about the preliminaries to the meeting "except that I was there early. It promised to be just an ordinary meeting until the audience really began to pile in. About the time the hall was fairly well filled, I left it on some errand or another. I never did get back in. Every seat in the ballroom was taken. Every inch of available standing room was taken. Then the fire department closed the doors and refused to allow anyone else to go in.

"The entrance to the ballroom was jammed solid by would-be listeners. The office was packed solid. So many people were outside the hotel trying to get in that a detail of policemen was sent to the Astor to keep the sidewalk open.

"What happened at the meeting I don't know, because I never got back in to find out. The crowd was so thick when I tried it that I just could not get through. I don't recall, either, how many enrollments we took, but my suspicion is it was very few, because of the crowd.

"The next morning, someone called up from the Hotel Astor and said in substance 'We are trying to operate a hotel and not a circus. We like the Carnegie organization very much, but we shall be obliged if you never come back.' We never did.

"The next meeting was held in the old Hippodrome building. Every seat in the pit and the first and second galleries was filled. Only about a hundred seats were vacant in the third balcony. I know this for a fact, because I observed most of the meeting from there. Somewhat over six thousand people attended.

"Dale and I have always disagreed as to the immediate results of that Hippodrome meeting. My contention has always been that we took two enrollments. Others have held that we took only one. At any rate, what happened was that the crowd was so enormous that when they left the hall, they swept would-be enrollers past the enrollment tables and out into the street. However, a vast number of people did enroll immediately after that Hippodrome meeting, and it was regarded as a success."

While the course was responsible for the book, rather than vice versa, when Carnegie died in 1955 his obituaries universally acclaimed him as the author of *How to Win Friends and Influence People.* The *New York Times* described the book as "one of the world's best sellers" which "made its author known wherever books are read." It was a tribute that would have pleased the farm boy from Missouri, for he went to his grave probably the most astonished author of his time.

A quarter-century after Carnegie wrote his epic best seller it still continues to sell at a lively pace of more than ten thousand copies a year, popping up in some of the most unexpected places to join hands with the Dale Carnegie Course in helping extraordinary individuals and groups to win friends and influence people.

12.

IN A SMALL ROOM at Michigan State Prison hangs the picture of an attractive woman with an overhead banner bearing this message: "Remember, Gentlemen, there is a lady present." The picture is of Dorothy Carnegie, and the room is where Dale Carnegie classes are held for inmates of the prison. Prison classrooms are the only places Carnegie classes are held where

AND
BEHIND BARS!

The Drama of Carnegie
Classes in Prisons

iron bars on the windows and guards at the door make it impossible for fear-stricken students to take to their heels.

Of all the special classes given by Dale Carnegie & Associates and their sponsors, none have been more successful and more eagerly received than those given to prisoners. In 1960 some fifteen hundred inmates of

231

thirty-one penal institutions in the United States and Canada completed work in forty-eight classes. More than seven thousand prisoners have participated since the prison program was initiated in Hawaii in 1950 by J. Edwin Whitlow, the Carnegie sponsor there.

These classes often have a poignancy and drama seldom found elsewhere. In a British Columbia penitentiary a few years ago a prisoner gave a human relations talk about what the course had done for him:

"Shortly after our first class, I had the opportunity to write my wife a letter. Bearing in mind the story told to us by Wal Angus (the Dale Carnegie sponsor-instructor in Victoria) at that time, I decided to put some of those ideas into practice. Now, I don't know about you fellows, but I myself sometimes find it difficult to write a very cheerful letter from here. However, this time I sat down and gave serious thought to what I could sincerely say in praise, and thanks, to my wife's difficult task of making a home for our children while I'm paying off my debt to society. It wasn't hard to find ground for praise. So here is the gist of my letter to her:

" 'Jean, I wonder if you realize how much I thank you for the marvelous care you are taking of our two daughters . . . I have always been rather hesitant to give praise, yet you may be sure that I give a great deal of thought to, and inwardly appreciate, how well you are doing a difficult job. The girls are very, very fortunate to have a mother who thinks so much of their welfare and happiness. I am fortunate, too, to have a wife who can tackle the job courageously, and, at the same time, seem to enjoy doing it. So much am I aware of your many thoughts and accomplishments, Jean, I'd love to tell them to you in person, along with a beautiful bouquet of flowers as a token of my appreciation. Well done, Jean! Well done! Thanks for sending the paper, thanks for your many letters, and thanks for looking after things so well.'

"That, fellows, was more or less the trend of my sincere appreciation. Certainly my wife deserves every word of it. Now here is the result of that letter: my wife's reply. Allow me to read a portion of it:

" '. . . Tonight I arrived home terribly tired from a hard day at work, and in a fit of depression hard to describe. I was wondering if all this hard work was worth while. Your letter had arrived, but I was so miserable, I must admit I put off reading it until I had the children tucked in bed. Then, after finishing the many household tasks, I sat down and opened your letter.

" 'Oh, darling! What a godsend that letter was! All at once the weariness and depression fell off me. I knew that someone thought that my hard work was worth the effort. You've no idea what your letter has done for me tonight! Although I do not really warrant all the praise you have given me, it makes me feel like a new person to know that someone appreciates. . . .' "

Since the prison classes were started, several Carnegie sponsors have fretted about what they may be doing to the organization's "image" in the public mind. Mrs. Carnegie, an enthusiastic supporter of the prison classes, took note of their attitude in an address at the Carnegie organization's international convention in 1958. She observed that "a number of our thoughtful sponsors" had not taken part in the prison program because of "the old objection: How is it going to affect public relations for our public classes to know that the same course of training is given inside prison walls to offenders against society?" To this objection she replied, "I want to say that my own personal opinion is that doing a thing that is good and worthy to be done never hurts anybody. I have no interest in anything when that ceases to be a fact."

From her weighty prison file, Mrs. Carnegie recited the reaction of several prison officials. Their comments ranged from a conservative statement that "the Carnegie courses do the most good where the greatest need exists," to enthusiasts who called the results "fantastic" and "electrifying." Penologists in both the United States and Canada have recommended that the courses should be made part of the correctional curriculum of every prison in the country.

A Texas prison executive wrote: "I am primarily concerned with the rehabilitation of inmates. In more than nine years in this profession, I have observed every conceivable means of attempting to achieve a spiritual awakening in men. We offer church, school, correspondence courses, organized recreation, vocational training, Alcoholics Anonymous groups, and numerous other character-development programs. None of these has approached the enormous impact of your course in self-improvement. I could not have believed some of the changes I have seen had I not known the men before they started the course. Hardened criminals, bitter, calloused, defeated men, have raised their heads in a new determination that they can pay their debts to society and then return to that society as useful, productive citizens.

"The Department of Correction is, in fact, benefiting as much as the inmates taking the course. Each class represents forty men circulating among the inmate population spreading good will and positive thinking. This makes all our jobs easier.

"Some of the students in prison classes have been taken to meetings of local civic groups, such as Lions Clubs and Rotary Clubs, to make talks on the Carnegie course and what it has meant to them. We are thrilled at the amazement expressed by those people at the sincerity and determination which is so evident in the inmates."

A Utah prison official stated that "we have watched men literally change from antisocial introverts to social extroverts."

The head of a military prison recommended the course "for other prisons and this without reservation. . . . I can tell you that the Dale Carnegie Course has, in my opinion, been responsible for bringing about model prisoner behavior in men who were previously severe disciplinary problems."

Mrs. Carnegie pointed out to her associates that studies showed the number of Carnegie students who returned to prison was much lower than the general average; recidivism of Carnegie students ranged from zero up to 22 per cent in different institutions, with an average of about 11 per cent, compared with normal prison recidivism ranging from 25 to 90 per cent and averaging about 50 per cent. In one federal reformatory it was figured that the cost of rearresting a man who broke parole or committed a new offense and had to be returned averaged about $8,200. In this one institution alone, it was estimated, the slashed recidivism rate saved taxpayers half a million dollars, not to mention the human values involved in salvaging the lives of these men.

The course is often heady stuff for prisoners; an inmate of Camp Pharsalia in New York, slated to be released, asked to be kept in custody long enough to take the course—a wish that was granted. A prisoner at Bordentown Reformatory in New Jersey, whose time was up just before his class was finished, got permission from prison authorities to return and complete the course. A student in a military prison in Leavenworth said, "This is the first time I have been praised for anything I have accomplished. My life has been one of constant blame or criticism for things in which I have failed."

What a prison class is like is touchingly related by an inmate at the Federal Correctional Institution at Terminal Island, San Pedro, California. Obviously trading on his own experience, he wrote:

"Way back as far as you care to remember, people have been trying to put the finger on the turning point, or most important time of their lives.

"This is the story of a young man who had offended society in such a way as to cause his peers to put him away for a period of time commensurate to the crime.

"He was shy when sober. A one-man entertainment

committee, and a raconteur when in his cups. He used the heady brew of the grain for a crutch. He was moody, temperamental, and like a cheap watch he needed a balance staff. He was plagued by fears. He had an abnormal fear of death and the hereafter. He left his friends holding their heads with his misdeeds. He fibbed to his friends, and he lied to himself. He either lived in the past, or tried to reach out and grab tomorrow. He was a hero in the dimly lit, exciting little bar that he frequented, and he was a bum in the sunlight. He was a number. He was in Limbo.

"He will henceforth be referred to as the Student.

"There were perhaps some more like him as the forty men crowded into the little room at the Federal Correctional Institution at Terminal Island, on a hot July evening in 1956. This was the opening of the Dale Carnegie Course. A neatly dressed, poised gentleman by the name of Larry Fawcett was on hand to greet each sinner. This was his first effort at bringing the course to a prison. He had probably never been in one before. Not as a guest and certainly not as a miscreant. Aiding him in the Crusade were three assistants.

"They, too, were faced with reality. The natives were restless. They engaged in frippery and banter, and the room sounded like a Chinese Kindergarten. He neared something that resembled order, and with that, made the announcement that as each man was called, he was to come to the front, face the motley crew, give his name, and tell why he was taking the course.

"The first few shambled up and went through the formality. It came the Student's turn. He blanched, he was reluctant. He looked wildly about for an escape. He was trapped in a device of his own making. In the vernacular of the street, 'he choked.' He was half carried, half pushed, to the podium by two large student goons. Mr. Fawcett felt moved to pose the question again. The Student studied the floor as if the answer were to come from there. He shifted, and scuffed his toes together like a small boy caught in a misdeed. He looked at the man as if he had asked for the Atomic Bomb Formula. He wished he were deep in the bowels of Alcatraz. Again the question, this time with a little more encouragement and compassion. Finally, and eyeing the floor again, the answer came out with all the volume of a cat crossing a velvet rug, 'My name is . . . ,' and as an afterthought he added, 'I wanna be able to get along with people.'

"The tide had turned, the sands had shifted; he went to his seat amid the tumultuous cheers of his obstreperous fellow sufferers. This was heady wine to him. This was the turning point. . . ."

The effect of the course, in his words, can't be measured by statistics. "Statistics are impossible in cases like these. How can we tell how many people we come into contact with, who knows how many lives will be richer and fuller by the lesson learned at Dale Carnegie? One thing is certain. Their lives here in prison have become more bearable. For out of the forty-odd in the class they carried a message to every inmate and official here. They reacted differently in times of stress. They became eager to listen to the other fellow in the face of disagreement. They made working conditions better, they followed orders cheerfully. They caused comment. If one wants statistics, they are not to be found here. They are in the musty ledgers, in the libraries and in the morgue."

How diverse the student body of prison classes is was suggested by a class recently given to twenty-five prisoners in Oregon State Penitentiary. The members included a former carnival worker, boxer, merchant seaman, golf caddiemaster, logger, accountant, race car driver, and others; some had been to college, others only to grammar school. Some were first offenders, others had long criminal records; their sentences ranged from two years to life and covered a variety of crimes. Some were described as model prisoners, others were labeled as problems. Several were war veterans; their ages ranged from 20 to more than 45. They represented a cross section of the prison population.

The course was made possible by prison authorities, working with Wellman and Blanche Pettit, Carnegie sponsors for Oregon and southern Washington, and their associate sponsor, Richard Wells. "I'm right at home here now," said Mrs. Pettit, who acted as graduate assistant. "They call me Sam."

A picturesque description of the setting of the class was given in *The Oregonian* (April 21, 1961): "The students sat on straight wooden chairs at one end of the prison chapel. The room was well-lit, with pale green walls punctuated by barred windows. Most wore blue work shirts and blue jeans, and several had little red booklets (the course outlines) stuffed in their hip pockets."

One prisoner in the class said at the final session, "I've gained enough from this course alone to keep me out of this penitentiary or any other."

From the beneficiaries of prison courses, Mrs. Carnegie has a trunk full of gifts . . . "and I treasure them," she said; they consist of embroidered handkerchiefs, jewelry boxes, leather work, and other tokens of appreciation made by inmates. There are also stacks of gratuitous testimonial letters and avowals of good intentions.

One of the big things prisoners get out of the training, Mrs. Carnegie says, is the ability to express themselves without profanity and obscenity. "No matter how articulate you are in that department, it is a limiting factor. It is a great release in a personality when a man learns he can express himself in a more socially acceptable way. Some are at a disadvantage when they go before the parole board. They are unable to speak for themselves. They are aware of this deficiency and this makes it even harder for them. No one can appreciate how difficult it is for these men to talk without being around them. You can feel it in your own muscles. When they do learn to speak, it is a psychological break-through.

"It also has a good effect because the course is given by people from the outside. For many men it is their only contact with the law-abiding element of society on an equal basis. The classes are the same as on the outside and the men are treated the same. Many start with a chip on their shoulder, looking for the gimmick; they can't believe that anybody is giving them anything without getting something out of it. When it finally dawns on them that there is no gimmick, they have tremendous respect for the instructors, and for the Carnegie organization.

"Often the prisoners are more tense and ingrown than people on the outside. They are tough in behavior, but inside themselves they are terrified."

Countless success stories are told about how the students fare after getting out of prison. C. I. Blackwood, who has taught more than a thousand inmates from twenty-five classes held at the federal reformatory in El Reno, Oklahoma, during the last decade, noted that one of the men who was serving a long sentence when he first met him is now in a sales job making $12,000 to $18,000 a year. "Another man who is still in prison took the course about a year ago, and it has helped him greatly in adjusting to prison life. Here are some of the things which . . . , Number 27076, told me had happened to him since he completed the Dale Carnegie class: elected president of the institution umpires' association, assistant manager of a softball team; staff writer for Plain Talk, the prison newspaper; umpire for one of the baseball leagues, as well as teaching an umpires' class." These may sound like small triumphs to one on the outside, but this is the prisoner's world, and these are his miracles.

Not all of the prisoners who complete the course and leave prison go on to triumph. Some end in disaster. The occasional disappointment is part of the risk. But prison officials are delighted with the ones who don't come back, and Carnegie people find their reward in the low recidivism rate of their students and the number who succeed in the outside world.

To help make the classes possible, Dale Carnegie & Associates furnish all supplies for prison classes without charge, and the sponsors and instructors donate their time. Instructors who teach the classes frequently become tremendously involved with the prisoners and their problems; many become father figures and serve as friend, adviser, and confidant. Most instructors of prison classes have large files of letters thanking them for what they have done, and they continue to get letters and cards—especially at Christmas—for many years. Blackwood always buys "my boys" their first meal on the outside after they are released.

William R. Cooley, a Carnegie instructor in Indianapolis, said that working with prisoners "has led me into a completely new and thrilling situation which has so completely engulfed my life that I now devote full time to working with inmates and parolees from prisons, including instructing many prison Dale Carnegie classes." He said that he became so engrossed in prison work that he has promoted a local organization called Prisoners' Aid by Citizen Effort

(PACE), with an office and full-time director and staff. "This has made such a profound change in my life that I feel my 66 years have been in preparation for the work ahead."

Cooley recalled his first prison class at the reformatory at Pendleton, Indiana. It was a cold winter night, "with only one guard who stood by the door while I went into the meeting room. There sat the group of inmates, all dressed alike, ready for the class to start. I was a little disconcerted that they seemed well fed, not as woebegone as I had expected, and they seemed slightly amused about something—probably what they were going to do to me.

"In this first class it turned out that there were several who had no interest whatever in Dale Carnegie. They wanted it on their packet that they had taken the course. They were shooting an angle—which is smart prison thinking. And I suppose they figured there was no harm in having some good clean fun with this old codger who obviously didn't know much about prison life.

"And what fun they proceeded to have. For their talks they would tell the wildest tales about rolling liquor stores and gasoline stations, or robbing a bank, or raping a woman, with all the details, and the class would cheer and yell and stomp the floor. And in

Dale Carnegie classes the instructor is required to find something on which to compliment the speaker. My instructor training hadn't covered this situation."

In the fifth session, when the prisoners were supposed to break out of their shells by using a shillelagh, Cooley said that "a few brought two *Life* magazines rolled tightly and taped the entire length. They would make a good ball bat. Or a club. During the evening they completely demolished two heavy office desks, and broke out a window. I lost eight pounds.

"But the Dale Carnegie technique got to them, and one by one they turned out to be just lonesome, mixed-up kids. One of the last to drop his shell was Don. . . . Don could tell the dirtiest tales, in the most interesting manner, and the class really enjoyed it. One night he was telling how he had always been clever, even as a kid. After his parents were divorced he had gone to live with a simple-minded old grandmother. She was just plain crazy about him and let him do just about as he pleased. When he was about 10 he found out where she kept her money. But he was smart. He didn't take all of it. Just a little at a time. And Grandma would fret about how forgetful she was getting. 'Boy, it was a scream,' he said.

"Don really was enjoying telling about it. But suddenly something seemed to jab him and almost in an undertone, he said, 'Seems like it was about that time I started hating her.' Then he went on with his tale. But more thoughts kept breaking in. 'I guess this was about when my trouble all started.' Then more big talk, and more of those interrupting thoughts, till his eyes filled with tears, and he had to sit down, crying. Here was their hero, no different from them. I think I realized for the first time the real force of the Dale Carnegie Course. . . . No amount of preaching could do what these men were doing for themselves.

"Perhaps it is human nature to think our lot is more difficult than anyone else's, and inmates are no different than the rest of us. In a Dale Carnegie class when they hear about the experiences of others, their own become less unique."

As a result of his exposure to the inmates' problems, Cooley said, "I was overwhelmed with the enormous problem of human lives being let go down the drain. I started searching for the answers. Although these men wanted out, it seemed that most of them had been out on parole at least once and were back. This didn't make sense. For the next year I prowled around the prison, learning details of operation. I helped set up Dale Carnegie classes in other prisons in order to study and compare prison populations. I joined many correctional associations including the

American Correction Association. . . . I have devoted much time to men out on parole. Jobs, diversion,
social contacts. . . . By boning up on psychology,
sociology, abnormal psychology, through university
extension courses and much research—but mostly by
trial and error, and much luck—I have been a part of
many mixed-up men's experiences in finding their way
back.

"Half of the men released from prison don't make
it. We don't need to look far for the reasons. Lack of
jobs, of course. But even deeper is the need for group
acceptance. A feeling of fitting into the scheme of
things. And at least some friendly association and diversion. The usual background of lack of love and
firm guidance in the early formative years has low-
ered their threshold of tolerance for the usual rebuffs,
especially when they are first released. It doesn't take
many turndowns to prove to them they aren't being
given a fair shake. And it's what they think that
counts."

Cooley concluded: "We demand better cars, television, and food—all designed to provide us with
better living. But half of our hospital beds are filled
with neurotic patients, and our prisons are bulging
with mixed-up, emotionally disturbed kids who are

not really criminals. I submit that it's time we placed some emphasis on the art, or science, of living."

Cooley's remarks could be enlarged to fit not only prisoners in penal institutions but people everywhere who are prisoners of themselves, prisoners of fear and repression and all the forces in modern life that keep them from realizing their full potential as human beings.

13.

Rededication to an Ideal

A LOOK
TO THE
FUTURE

THIS, THEN, is the story of the Dale Carnegie Course as it has evolved from its modest start at the 125th Street YMCA in New York in 1912. Since that memorable date when Dale Carnegie began his revolutionary method of teaching public speaking, almost one million persons have taken the training and gone forth to spread its fame. Today Carnegie graduates can be found in every state of the Union and in virtually every nation throughout the world.

The preceding chapters have noted that these graduates come from every possible type of background and represent every economic and social stratum, but they all have one thing in common—to better themselves in some respect. Their goals may differ in degree or kind, but basically they want more money; greater social or professional stature; ability to get along better with their neighbors and business associates; freedom from fear and worry; capacity to feel more comfortable in social situations. In a word, they believe that life has more to offer than they are getting, and they are determined to find greater fulfillment by making the most of their God-given abilities and talents. When they enroll in the Carnegie course they have taken an important first step toward achieving this goal.

During the fourteen weeks the course lasts, the students are inexorably linked together as they share a common experience and, by helping one another, work toward reshaping their lives.

The Dale Carnegie Course, as noted previously, does not promise miracles, but it does promise, and it delivers, concrete results in helping people to help themselves, in bringing them in fuller contact with other people and with life itself.

While the Carnegie organization is fundamentally a

commercial enterprise, throughout its make-up runs a strong thread of dedication to the human ideal. The men and women who operate the various franchises and teach the classes are bound by an unusual and highly developed sense of obligation to help the students achieve their individual goals.

Dale Carnegie expressed what he hoped to achieve for those who took the course when he told his graduate assistants:

"As you start on this exciting experience I sincerely believe we can all experience a heaven on this earth, if we can devote our lives to giving—rather than getting. We can come to know untold joy, peace, contentment, and happiness by helping others to get what they want. Let's do what we can to erase from this world the handicaps of selfishness, dishonesty, malice, jealousy, intolerance, pessimism, depression, fear and worry. Let's do our best to replace them with love, patience, kindness, intelligence, ability, tolerance, peace, self-confidence, and freedom from fear and worry.

"Accomplish this and you will have gained and shared your most priceless fortune."

Since Dale Carnegie wrote those words a few years before his death, the ideals and aims of the course have not changed. Methods and teaching techniques have been altered to meet changing times, and improved whenever possible, but the course is still rooted in working with and for the individual student in his search for new and broader horizons.

On its fiftieth anniversary the Carnegie organization, led by its president, Dorothy Carnegie, paused to evaluate its position, its progress, and to rededicate itself to the ideal of service that inspired its founder and those who have carried on the Carnegie tradition.

This book is the expression of that rededication, and through it the entire Carnegie organization pays tribute to the people who have enabled it to prosper materially and spiritually—those who have taken the Carnegie training in order to find for themselves, and for those they live and associate with, a richer and fuller life.